the BOOK

OF the

VEDAS

THE
BOOK
OF THE
VEDAS

VIRENDER KUMAR ARYA

EDITED BY MALCOLM DAY

BARRON'S

A QUARTO BOOK

First edition for the United States,
its territories and dependencies
and Canada, published in 2003 by
Barron's Educational Series, Inc.
All inquiries should be addressed to:
Barron's Educational Series, Inc.
250 Wireless Boulevard
Hauppauge, New York 11788
http://www.barronseduc.com

International Standard Book No. 0-7641-5597-0
Library of Congress Catalog Card No. 2002106720

QUAR.TBV
Conceived, designed, and produced by
Quarto Publishing plc
The Old Brewery
6 Blundell Street
London N7 9BH

Project Editors: Fiona Robertson, Tracie Lee Davis
Designer and Art Editor: Elizabeth Healey
Editor: Andrew Armitage
Illustrator: Julian Baker
Proofreader: Anne Plume
Indexer: Diana Le Core
Art Director: Moira Clinch
Publisher: Piers Spence

Manufactured by
Universal Graphics Pte Ltd, Singapore
Printed in China by
Midas Printing International Ltd

9 8 7 6 5 4 3 2 1

contents

INtRODUCtION

The ancient literature known as the Vedas is sacred
to Hindus. Its hymns, prayers, and mystical writings
provide the scriptural foundation of their faith. Later
writings augment this ancient authority and in some
cases recast it for new generations, but it is the Vedic
worldview as a whole that the outsider must regard in
trying to fathom the essence of Hinduism.

The seemingly endless variety of images that
Hinduism presents to the enquirer can be bewildering.
A cross-legged ascetic, an ornate temple, a materialistic
householder, holy cremation beside the Ganges, animal-
headed gods—all have their place in Hinduism. There
is no founder, no single scripture or creed in this

religion. There are many gods but there is only one ultimate reality. Hinduism resists neat definitions and rejoices in diversity.

Perhaps the only way of describing this most complex of religions is as the sum of practices and beliefs of well over one billion Hindus living in the Indian subcontinent and other parts of the world today.

A key factor in the development of Hinduism in India has been its insulation from the rest of the world. Safe behind the natural barriers of sea and mountain, the faith turned inward in pursuit of spiritual harmony.

THE QUEST FOR INNER PEACE
LOOKING INTO THE SOUL

Arrival of the Aryans in India (*c.* 1500 B.C.E.)

B.C.E.	3000	2500	2000	1500	1000

Indus Valley Civilization
(*c.* 3500–1500 B.C.E.)

Development of the Vedas
(*c.* 1500–*c.* 800 B.C.E.)

The Himalayas to the north of India and the Indian Ocean, which engulfs its southern shores, have been effective deterrents to most would-be colonizers. Even when conquest did occur, under Muslim and British rules, it had little effect at the grassroots level on traditional Hindu society.

With no fear of displacement by outsiders, with nothing to threaten its stability, Hinduism became a religion at ease with itself. Unlike other world faiths, it did not search for a promised land; there were no prayers to be released from enslavement; there was no need of a messianic figure to usher in a heavenly kingdom on earth. Hindu society was settled in a rigid, stratified system, in which its members lived and died according to their rank. Patterns of life continued unchanged for countless generations. If people experienced anxiety or frustration with their lot in life, no one blamed an external influence or sought to change society, for society was ordered according to the law of divine nature.

Therefore, the Hindu way to resolve inner tensions is to look within oneself and make the necessary adjustments. There developed in Hinduism a number of techniques of self-control aimed at restoring peace of mind and harmony with the world. The goal for Hindus became this mastery of mind and emotion. Whoever can negate passion, desire, fear, and anger—the forces that militate against tranquility—will be set on the path to spiritual salvation.

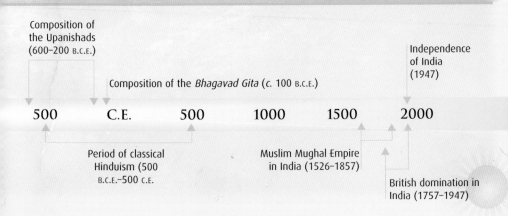

Composition of the Upanishads (600–200 B.C.E.)

Composition of the *Bhagavad Gita* (c. 100 B.C.E.)

Independence of India (1947)

| 500 | C.E. | 500 | 1000 | 1500 | 2000 |

Period of classical Hinduism (500 B.C.E.–500 C.E.

Muslim Mughal Empire in India (1526–1857)

British domination in India (1757–1947)

THE ROOTS OF THE RELIGION PRACTICED BY HINDUS TODAY
GO BACK TO THE BRILLIANT CIVILIZATION THAT EXISTED IN
THE INDUS VALLEY FROM ABOUT 3500 TO 1500 B.C.E.

THE INDUS VALLEY CIVILIZATION

EARLY INHABITANTS OF INDIA

Hinduism as it is followed today developed mainly during the first thousand years of the common era, but its origins can be traced back as far as 3500 B.C.E., the earliest date given for the civilization of the Indus Valley. Aryan peoples who invaded northwest India in about 1500 B.C.E. incorporated some of the beliefs and practices of the Indus Valley people into their own religion; and this fusion of the religion of the Aryans with the beliefs and practices of the Indus Valley, conveyed through the scriptures of the Aryans—the Vedas—is one of the cornerstones of Hinduism.

In the early 1920s, archaeologists who had been excavating in the Indus Valley, at Mohenjo Daro and Harappa, established that an advanced civilization had flourished there. The script of the Indus people, which was found on soapstone seals,

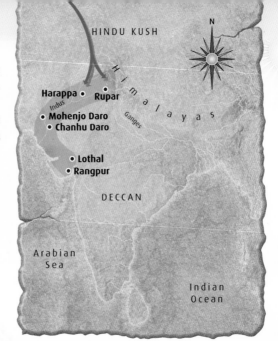

RIGHT When Aryan migrants crossed the Hindu Kush c. 1500 B.C.E., they found a civilization larger than contemporary Egypt already established in the Indus river valley (now in Pakistan).

HINDU KUSH

N

Harappa • Rupar •

Indus

• Mohenjo Daro
  • Chanhu Daro

Himalayas

Ganges

• Lothal
  • Rangpur

DECCAN

Arabian
Sea

Indian
Ocean

has not yet been deciphered, so all our information about their culture is based on the evidence of their material remains.

Although no place of worship has been unearthed at the Indus sites, depictions on the seals tell us something about the people's religious beliefs. For example, one seal shows a female figure nursing a baby, and perhaps represents a form of the Mother Goddess, a goddess found in most ancient cultures. The god Shiva, who has become one of the major deities in the Hindu pantheon, may be prefigured on seals that depict a god surrounded by animals. One seal shows him in a cross-legged posture, suggesting that yoga meditation, which forms such an important part of Hindu practice, has its roots in the Indus civilization.

LEFT Later Hindu deities such as Kali, grim consort of Shiva, may have been prefigured in the Indus civilization.

BACKGROUND Mohenjo Daro, along with Harappa, was one of the two great cities of this civilization.

THE ARYANS, AN UNSOPHISTICATED BUT SKILLFUL PEOPLE
FROM CENTRAL ASIA, WERE THE FOUNDING ELDERS OF THE
GREAT HINDU HYMNS OF SCRIPTURE KNOWN AS THE VEDAS.

ARYAN INVADERS

THE VEDIC AGE

ABOVE The Aryans brought to India their veneration of gods who personified elements of nature,
such as the fire deity, Agni.

The demise of the Indus civilization happened about the same time the region was invaded by a tribal people called the Aryans. Whereas the beliefs of the Indus people are known only from archaeological finds, those of the Aryans come down to us from the Vedas, the most ancient of the Hindu scriptures.

The Aryan, or Indo-European, newcomers were a tall, fair-skinned people believed to have migrated from central Asia in about 2000 B.C.E. One group settled in northern Greece and another in Iran (whose name is derived from "Aryan"); those who eventually entered India probably split off from the Iranian branch. Knowledge of the Aryans is derived mostly from the heritage of their sacred literature, the Vedas, especially the *Rig Veda*, a collection of hymns.

Originally hunters and nomads herding cattle, the Aryans were less sophisticated than their city-dwelling predecessors, but superior in metallurgy and weaponry. Once they had seized the land, they set down roots and became farmers. The Aryans spoke an early form of Sanskrit and organized themselves into tribes, subdivided into family clans. People started to form themselves into occupational groups, sowing the seeds of the later Hindu caste system.

The Aryans worshiped nature gods (see "The Vedas," page 20), making ritual offerings in the hope of obtaining good harvests. As a result of contact with the Indus people, the Aryans gradually adopted new deities, including the Mother Goddess, and probably the idea of ritual purity, the need to be "clean," both in body and spirit, before worship. In time, they intermarried with the indigenous inhabitants and gradually extended their settlements toward the Ganges Valley. By 1000 B.C.E., the Aryan culture had become predominant in northern India.

THE PERIOD FROM 500 B.C.E. to 500 C.E. saw the establishment in India of classical Hinduism, which became the basis of today's religion. The formation of Hinduism grew out of turbulent times in India, when invasions of outsiders and breakaway cults from within threatened the cohesion of society.

THE AGE OF CLASSICAL HINDUISM

THE RISE OF THE BRAHMINS

With Hindu society under threat from invaders such as the White Huns from central Asia, and from breakaway cults such as Buddhism and Jainism, the priestly aristocracy of India (the Brahmins) seized the opportunity to assert their authority as sole guardians of the faith. As the educated elite, the Brahmins were the only people who could read and write Sanskrit, the language of sacred scripture, and they were therefore well placed to establish a sense of religious orthodoxy, a right way for Hindus to conduct their lives. In so doing, they also imposed a keen sense of social order. As society expanded with foreign peoples and increased trade, new subclasses emerged. It was during this period that

LEFT Through the Purana scriptures, the Brahmins emphasized dutiful behavior, not meditation, as the true way of devotion to God.

BELOW A Brahmin prepares ritual offerings at a lakeside in Pushkar in India.

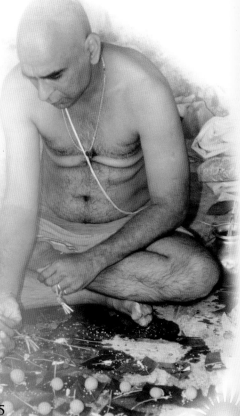

we see the fuller development of the caste system, one of Hindu India's most distinctive and enduring features.

With the rise of what is known as Brahminical Hinduism came a corresponding decline in the Vedic cult, with its emphasis on ritual sacrifices to the gods. Instead, more importance was attached to the quest for liberating the soul, as outlined in the Upanishads, the last work of the Vedas. A further refinement of Hindu ideals developed in the form of *bhakti*, devotion to a god based on love. This movement became especially prominent from the Middle Ages, and may have occurred as a result of influence from mystical Islam, especially when the Mughals held power in India, from 1526 to 1857.

15

HINDUISM IN MODERN INDIA

FROM COLONIZATION TO INDEPENDENCE

PERMANENT EUROPEAN SETTLEMENT IN INDIA BEGAN WHEN THE PORTUGUESE LANDED ON THE SOUTHWEST COAST IN 1498 AND TRADING POSTS WITH THE WEST WERE ESTABLISHED. BUT IT WAS NOT UNTIL THE BRITISH, UNDER ROBERT CLIVE, TOOK POWER IN 1757 THAT EUROPEAN COLONIZATION BECAME A REALITY AND INTRODUCED NEW INFLUENCES TO HINDUISM.

The British Raj (rule) lasted until 1947. The Indian encounter with Christianity, along with Western technology and ideas about society and education, led to reform within Hinduism, inspired largely by charismatic individuals such as Ram Mohan Roy, Dayanandi Sarasvati, Sri Ramakrishna, and Mohandas (Mahatma) Gandhi.

Ram Mohan Roy (1772–1833), a Bengali Brahmin, was influenced by Christianity. He founded the Brahma Samaj (Brahma Society), which stressed monotheism (belief in one god) and led social reforms, such as the abolition of child marriage and the immolation of widows *(sati)*. The reforms of Dayanandi Sarasvati (1824–83), a Brahmin from Gujarat, returned Hinduism to the purity of the Vedas, which were for him the source of all knowledge, including Western science. He founded the Arya Samaj, a society still active today, which denounced caste and promoted the education of women.

Sri Ramakrishna (1836–86) was a poor Bengali Brahmin whose mystic visions convinced him that God can be found through any religion. His most famous disciple was Swami Vivekananda (see "Swami Vivekananda," page 118).

Mahatma Gandhi (1869–1948), described as India's Great Soul, is revered as both an astute politician and a charismatic holy man. His campaign (from 1914 to 1947) of nonviolent protest against the Raj was based on the principle that God is also present in the hearts of wrongdoers, and that believers should seek to awaken that inner voice in their oppressors.

Since Indian independence in 1947, Hinduism has continued to evolve (see "Modern Hindu Cults," page 124), a trend which the reactionary Hindu political party Bharatiya Janata endeavors to prevent.

LEFT Gandhi, more than any other religious figure, helped to bring the Hindu soul of India into the modern era.

BACKGROUND The proclamation of Queen Victoria as Empress of India in 1876 did nothing to endear Hindu nationalists who wished for liberation from foreign rule.

CHAPTER 2

HOLY WRITINGS

Most of the Hindu scriptures were originally stored simply in the memories of priests. By special methods of memorization, religious poetry was passed from generation to generation orally before finally being written down (the earliest manuscript of the *Rig Veda* dates from about 1400 C.E., more than 2,000 years after its original formulation). The Aryans had no system of writing, but the fact that these scriptures remained in the oral tradition for so long has much to do with the delight and honor in which their recitation was (and still is) held.

When the revealed knowledge was written down, the language used was Sanskrit, a member of the Indo-European family. Its literature became the official vehicle of expression of Hindu society. There were two main periods of Sanskrit literature: the Vedic period, from 1500 to 500 B.C.E., and the period of classical Hinduism, from *c.* 500 B.C.E. to 500 C.E.

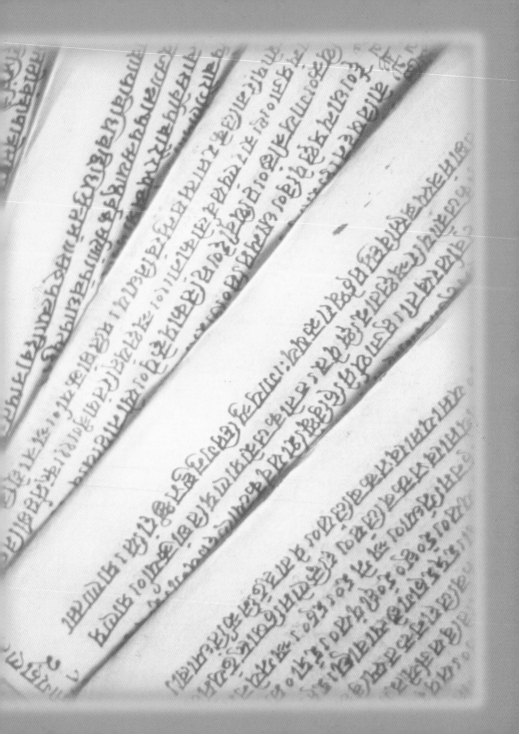

THE VEDAS (I)

ANCIENT SCRIPTURES OF THE ARYANS

THE VEDAS ARE FOUR COLLECTIONS OF SACRED HYMNS. IN ANCIENT TIMES THEY WERE BELIEVED TO HAVE BEEN REVEALED DIRECTLY, BY SPOKEN WORD, TO ARYAN SAGES AND WERE THEREFORE CALLED *SHRUTI*, MEANING "THAT WHICH IS HEARD."

ABOVE Like Vishnu, Surya was an early Vedic god of the sun. The two lotus flowers he carries symbolize the world beyond, where the sun resides, and this world, upon which he shines.

Passed down orally from one generation to the next, the Vedas were preserved by guilds of priests who had the special responsibility of performing rituals in which the hymns were recited. The most important of the four collections is the *Rig Veda* (meaning, in Sanskrit, the "praise wisdom"), which comprises 1,028 hymns organized into ten divisions, or "books." At key moments during a ritual, the priest would recite one or more of these hymns in praise of the Aryan gods, most of whom were believed to embody natural phenomena. The sun, ocean, rivers, hills, and dawn were all worshiped as deities.

The religion revealed by the Vedas indicates the early belief that the many gods together made up a complex and unified whole, in which they depended on each other to maintain the order, or symmetry, of existence. This symmetry, in turn, could be maintained only if human society—which was thought to reflect the system of the gods—performed sacrifices in strict accordance with the manner prescribed in the Vedas. As a result, there developed an elaborate system of ritual, which played a vital role in Vedic religion.

The second and third collections, the *Sama Veda* and *Yajur Veda*, deal entirely with ritual matters—the one an anthology of song and music to accompany sacrifices, the other a guide to other aspects of ceremonial practices. The fourth collection is the *Atharva Veda*, a body of knowledge for the use of a domestic medicine man.

Offerings made to the gods were believed to confer wealth and happiness to society. The early Vedic religion, therefore, was very "this-worldly," with little of the cosmology that developed in later, classical Hinduism.

ABOVE The Brahmin priests played a vital role in maintaining order in early Indian society.

IN the vedic age, hinduism was only just beginning its
philosophical quest into the nature of the spiritual
world. But many of the ideas that evolved in the
belief system of classical hinduism had their
origins in the vedas.

THE VEDAS (II)
THE ARYAN WORLDVIEW

The *atman* was already understood to be one's soul,
a subtle substance essential to existence that dwelled
in the body. Yet, on death, this life breath left the
body to rise in the smoke of the funeral pyre to heaven,
which lay above the atmosphere. As long as the rituals were
correctly performed on earth, people from the Vedic age fully
expected to continue a pleasurable life in heaven, where
they would live with their ancestors in eternal light.

The Vedas portray an understanding of the universe as
existing on three levels. The lowest was the earthly realm,
where humans and animals lived; then came the
atmosphere, in which birds flew and the gods might
sometimes be seen; above the vault of the sky was the
heavenly realm, where the gods lived with the dead.

In the Vedas comes the forerunner of the great Hindu
concepts of *dharma*, the principle of right living, and

BACKGROUND Pilgrims massing at Allahabad for the ancient festival of Kumbha Mela (see page 114).

Brahman, the universal spirit. Known as *rita*, it is the impersonal principle that governs the universe and gives it its order and rhythm. The daily rising and setting of the sun, the yearly seasons, the consistent pattern of growth and decay, all result from rita.

Yet this principle is no God, as would be conceived in later Hinduism. All that was seen in the world—creatures, humanity, even the gods themselves—came into being as a result of this original principle, as the Hymn of Creation from the *Rig Veda* asserts:

> Neither death nor immortality was there then; there was no distinction of night and day. That One breathed without breath by inner power . . . by the might of its own fervor That One was born. (Book 10, 129:2–3)

ABOVE Pilgrims dedicated to Shiva making their way to a temple for worship.

THE
UPANISHADS
THE HIMALAYAS OF THE SOUL

Composed between 600 and 200 B.C.E., the Upanishads are one of the world's great spiritual texts. Their breadth of thought, profound insights, and evocative language have attracted mystics, philosophers, and poets from the time of their inception to the modern era. The German philosopher Arthur Schopenhauer (1788–1860), for example, said that reading them "has been the consolation of my life, and will be of my death."

ABOVE The Vedic god Rudra, also known as "the Howler," was the god of destruction who evolved into Shiva.

Although this slim collection of Sanskrit verses embodies a new religious faith with its own approach to the problems of life, it is regarded as a culmination of the entire Vedic tradition, and was called the Vedanta, meaning "End of the Vedas." The texts consist of mystical dialogues between teacher and pupil, or between sages. Although there are more than a hundred such dialogues from different periods, only thirteen are accepted by all Hindus as true scripture.

Their name meaning "secret teaching," the Upanishads are not intended for the casual inquirer. Their truth can be understood only by those with a special attitude of mind. One of their main teachings is that the power of *maya* ("illusion") makes the world appear real, but Brahman (the world soul) is the ultimate reality. People possess an individual soul or spirit (atman), which is indestructible and capable of fusing with Brahman. The atman's future existence is determined by *karma* (the result of all actions), and the atman can achieve liberation *(moksha)* from the long cycle of birth and rebirth, known as *samsara,* a concept first outlined in the Upanishads. Whereas the earlier Vedic hymns showed little concern with the afterlife, there is now much greater preoccupation with the problem of this endless cycle of birth and rebirth.

The authors of the Upanishads were more than religious philosophers. They were mystics who, by stimulating imagination and intuition, hoped to enable the faithful to see visions of Brahman, the hidden power latent in all creation.

See also "Raja Yoga," "Hatha Yoga," "Laya Yoga," and "Mantra Yoga" (which all derive from the Upanishads), pages 74–81.

WITH THE RISE IN IMPORTANCE OF THE UPANISHADS, WHICH REPRESENTED A MOVEMENT AWAY FROM WORLDLY LIVING TOWARD MORE SPIRITUAL CONCERNS, CAME THE SIMULTANEOUS NEED FELT BY THE PRIESTLY CLASS (THE BRAHMINS) TO ESTABLISH A CODE OF LAW. THIS CODE BECAME FUNDAMENTAL TO THE HINDU WAY OF LIFE.

THE DHARMA SUTRAS AND DHARMA SHASTRAS
LAWS FOR LIVING

RIGHT A sadhu, or holy man, studies a philosophical guide to correct living.

As new sects, such as Buddhism and Jainism, and new social classes, such as merchants, emerged in the centuries between 500 B.C.E. and 500 C.E., the Brahmins made it their duty to lay down codes of conduct, both moral and ritual.

The Dharma Sutras and Dharma Shastras were law books compiled so that Hindus of every caste and stage of life would know how to behave. The Dharma Sutras were inspired by the Vedas and were later elaborated into the more systematic Dharma Shastras, which became the basis of modern Hindu law. One Shastra in particular, known as the Law of Manu (the equivalent of Noah for Jews and Christians), became preeminent.

This body of law covered every aspect of life, from diet to funerary customs. Because it prescribed codes of conduct for each of the four *varnas* (social strata in Hindu society—see "Caste," page 94) as well as for the four stages of life (student, householder, recluse, or ascetic), the work was enormously complex. It included eight forms of marriage, rites of initiation, rules about purification and pollution, etiquette for women,

guides to hospitality, and a host of explanations about the more philosophical doctrines of Hinduism, such as karma, the soul, and sin.

Underlying the laws outlined in the Dharma Shastras were three aims in life: the earning of religious merit through correct living, the lawful making of wealth, and *kama*, the satisfaction of desires.

27

IN EARLY MEDIEVAL INDIA the important PURANAS were COMPOSED. These were myths and legends glorifying the gods, especially BRAHMA, VISHNU, and SHIVA. Written in verse, they are a treasure trove of folklore and wisdom, with topics that include the periodic destruction and rebirth of the world, and the genealogy of HINDU gods and heroes.

THE PURANAS
FOLKLORE ABOUT THE DEITIES

ABOVE Krishna and his brother Balarama, here dressed as cowherds, are the subjects of many Indian folk tales.

28

They are closely linked with the great epics of Indian literature, the *Mahabharata* and *Ramayana*, and became vehicles for the religious beliefs and worship of the Hindu masses. The eighteen principal Puranas and numerous local variations describe the adventures of their gods and goddesses. Through the stories, devotees understand the past and the present, as well as receive reassurance that they are participating in a preordained divine plan. The deities are brought closer to the lives of the people by manifesting human characteristics: the loving, the wrathful, the jealous, and the forgiving traits found in male and female deities portray a universe in which good and evil compete to exert influence over human souls.

By far the most popular text is the *Bhagavata Purana*, which tells of the life of Krishna. Its emphasis on recounting the exploits of his youth—the threats on his life made by the tyrant Kamsa, his flight from the cowherds at Gokula, and especially his pranks with the cow maidens—has made the text a classic. Many medieval Indian paintings were inspired by these stories.

An important aspect of the Puranas is the devotion shown to the deities. In return for the service rendered by the gods, worshipers are expected to serve them by performing ritual sacrifices and by living according to the laws (the Sutras and Shastras) prescribed for their caste.

THE RAMAYANA EPIC

LEGEND IN POETRY

The *Ramayana* is one of two great Sanskrit epics in Indian literature. It is a poetic rendering of various myths and legends that, over the course of four or five centuries around the start of the common era, was expanded to take on a more specifically religious view in support of Brahminical Hinduism.

ABOVE The blessed Prince Rama and his wife Sita take on the demon king of Lanka in an epic struggle of good versus evil.

I n 24,000 verses, arranged in seven books, the *Ramayana* tells the story of Prince Rama. It relates how Rama marries Sita, the daughter of King Janaka, after winning an archery contest. However, the prince's fortunes change when his rightful claim as heir to King Dasharatha's throne is disregarded and he is exiled to a forest with Sita and his brother, Lakshmana.

During the exile, Sita is kidnapped by Ravana, demon king of Lanka (Sri Lanka). With the help of the king of the monkeys, Sugriva, and his monkey general, Hanuman, Rama crosses the sea with an army of monkeys and attacks Lanka. In a final battle Ravana is killed, Sita is rescued, and Rama is later restored to his kingdom.

But, although the gods rejoice in Ravana's destruction, Rama is suspicious of Sita's conduct when she was a prisoner. To prove her innocence she calls a public witness. Sita, whose name means a "furrow," is received by Mother Earth, who, by opening up and taking her in, proves Sita's goodness.

Unable to endure life without Sita, the disconsolate Rama follows her into eternity by plunging into a river.

The epic portrays ideals of human virtue: by destroying the demon Ravana, Rama restores righteousness to the earth. He himself embodies the obedient son, loving husband, dutiful king, and affectionate brother. Hanuman is the ideal servant and Sita the ideal faithful wife.

RIGHT The marriage of Rama and Sita.

Eight times as long as the *Iliad* and the *Odyssey* together, and more than three times the size of the Bible, India's great epic is the most sustained act of storytelling in world literature.

THE
MAHABHARATA
EPIC

A LONG JOURNEY WITH MANY DETOURS

ABOVE The characters and sub-plots in the *Mahabharata* provide an endless source of material for Indian television costume dramas.

The name *Mahabharata* means "Great [story of the] Bharatas." It tells of the conflict between two branches of the Bharata family, the Kauravas and the Pandavas, culminating in an eighteen-day war. The word *Bharata* is also used metaphorically for the Indian race, so the *Mahabharata* is sometimes referred to as "the great story of India." Of its 100,000 two-line verses, only about 4,000 relate to the main story: the rest contain additional myths and teachings. In other words, the *Mahabharata* resembles a long journey with many detours. It is said that "Whatever is here is found elsewhere. But whatever is not here is nowhere else."

It is impossible to give a precise date for the creation of the *Mahabharata*—it was composed by anonymous poets over many generations—but it was probably formulated between the fourth and second centuries B.C.E., and handed down orally until written down around 300 C.E. In addition to being a gripping family-feud saga, the *Mahabharata* is a fount of religious and moral knowledge. One of its central doctrines is that of the avatars (see "Avatars," page 56), the incarnation of the Hindu gods in human form. The incarnate gods are not the impersonal forces of nature of the earlier Vedas, nor the abstract godhead of the Upanishads, but beings of flesh and blood who interact directly with humans.

Like Shakespeare, the *Mahabharata* is a linguistic storehouse that has been raided extensively by writers and poets. Its plotlines were retold for centuries by traveling storytellers and puppeteers, and now feature in countless television dramas and Bollywood epics.

BELOW A ceremonial unveiling in a banquet scene from the epic.

THE *BHAGAVAD GITA*, A MODEST TEXT OF 700 VERSES ARRANGED IN EIGHTEEN CHAPTERS, IS ARGUABLY THE MOST POPULAR AND WIDELY REVERED OF ALL HINDU SCRIPTURES. SCHOLARS BELIEVE IT WAS ADDED TO THE SIXTH BOOK OF THE EPIC *MAHABHARATA* TO PROMOTE BRAHMINICAL HINDUISM AND THE WORSHIP OF KRISHNA.

BHAGAVAD GITA (I)

THE BOOK OF KRISHNA

Set before the final battle between the two warring families, the *Gita* relates how Arjuna, one of the Pandavas, revolts at the idea of having to kill his kinsmen. Krishna, Arjuna's charioteer and an incarnation of Vishnu, argues that Arjuna should follow his duty as a noble and fight.

The book goes on to explore the nature of atman and Brahman, and the paths of liberation (moksha). It also describes the moral and religious duties of the four varnas (social categories), and examines the concept of desireless action.

Krishna, as an incarnation of Vishnu, is the supreme deity and object of devotion in the *Gita*, and his answers to Arjuna's questions are believed by many Hindus to be the word of God. Lord Krishna speaks of three routes to salvation: by enlightenment *(jnana)*; by right action (karma); and, best of all, by loving devotion to the Lord (the practice of bhakti).

The way of enlightenment involves discerning what is real from what is unreal. Wrong perception or illusion (maya) prevents people from reaching the part of themselves that is immortal. The way of karma is to follow one's true path (dharma) by behaving in a way appropriate to one's birth (see "Dharma," page 66). Actions must be carried out without desire or attachment to the outcome, so that one can engage in the world but not be controlled by it. The way of loving devotion involves a total surrender to God. Through meditations, prayer, and repetition of God's name, the worshiper awaits the divine bestowal of grace as the means to salvation.

ABOVE Lord Krishna, on horseback, guides Arjuna to fulfill his duty in fighting for a noble cause.

BACKGROUND An eighteenth-century Indian manuscript of the *Bhagavad Gita*.

LORD KRISHNA AND ARJUNA'S DISCUSSION OF THE STRATEGY FOR DEFEATING THEIR RIVALS IN BATTLE IS AN ALLEGORY OF THE PERSONAL STRUGGLE FOR LIBERATION (MOKSHA). THE EARTHLY FOE REPRESENTS THE ENEMY OF THE HUMAN SOUL AND THE MILITARY STRATEGY IS THE INDIVIDUAL'S QUEST FOR SPIRITUAL SALVATION.

BHAGAVAD GITA (II)
THE WAY TO LIBERATION

Driven by the fear of unhappiness and attracted by the promise of happiness (liberation), Arjuna comes to see that "delights are wombs of *dukkha* [suffering]" (5:22) and that the wise man is "not perturbed by dukkha" (6:23) for he understands that atman (soul) exists in everything, that therefore pleasure and suffering have the same result, namely they bind the self to worldly existence.

> He whose mind is undisturbed though immersed in dukkha [suffering], who is indifferent to *sukkha* [pleasure], for whom all passions, fears and hatreds have departed, such a man is a *muni* [ascetic sage] of steady mind. (2:56)

There are two principal causes of suffering: desire or lust (kama) and ignorance *(ajnana)*. Other causes, such as hatred and greed, exist but are thought really to stem from desire. Arjuna asks Krishna what makes someone do evil, which brings suffering and unhappiness. Krishna replies:

It is lust, it is hatred, born of the *guna* [strand] of passion, all devouring, all polluting, that is the enemy, that is your real foe here on earth . . . Lust, the ever present enemy of the wise man, envelops true knowledge like an unquenchable fire. (3:37, 39)

The route to salvation is to practice the various methods of yoga exercise, which the wise person understands will eliminate all causes of suffering. See also "Jnana Yoga," "Karma Yoga," and "Bhakti Yoga," pages 84–89.

RIGHT An ascetic may practice extreme forms of yoga in his bid to overcome the causes of suffering and thereby find salvation.

LEFT Krishna mastered the unsettling influences of passion, fear, and anger.

THE HINDU PANTHEON

CHAPTER
3

"There is one God but many gods" is a common maxim applied to Hindus' understanding of the divine, a mixture of monotheism and pantheism. While believing there is only one supreme God, Hindus may worship any number of subordinate gods or spiritual powers, regarded as manifestations of the one God and often endowed with specialized functions.

At the head of the Hindu pantheon is the Trimurti, the trinity of Brahma (the creator), Vishnu (the preserver), and Shiva (the destroyer and regenerator). All three gods are considered to be aspects of Brahman, the one God or universal soul described in the Upanishads. Female deities also play important roles. Each of the three gods has a consort in classical Hinduism. A key figure in worship today is the Mother Goddess, Devi.

THE FIRST MEMBER OF THE HINDU TRINITY—WHICH ALSO
CONTAINS VISHNU THE PRESERVER AND SHIVA THE
DESTROYER—HAS HAD A SURPRISINGLY SHADOWY PAST
COMPARED WITH HIS TWO ILLUSTRIOUS COUNTERPARTS.

BRAHMA

LORD AND FATHER
OF ALL CREATION

B rahma does not figure at all in the early Vedic scriptures. By the beginning of the classical period of Hinduism, near the time of Jesus Christ, he became identified with the creator god of the *Rig Veda*. But he has since lost his creative powers to Shiva and Vishnu, as well as to the great goddess Devi, and receded into the background of the pantheon. Since his sole interest is the overall structure of the universe, it is said that he has left the less pleasant tasks, such as combating evil, to Vishnu and Shiva.

According to Hindu creation mythology, the primeval essence, or Brahman, made the cosmic waters and deposited a seed in them. The seed became a golden egg, which was reborn as Brahma, from whom all creation issues. The first creature was the Cosmic Man, one of Brahma's names, and Brahma is regarded as the first and greatest of all sages.

Red in color, he has four faces, which represent the four Vedas, the four epochs of time, and the four social categories of caste (varnas), and his four arms are the four quarters of the universe. He also has a rosary, which controls time, a book containing all knowledge, and a water pot representing the waters of creation.

ABOVE According to one legend, Brahma issued from the navel of the god Vishnu as he reclined on a lotus flower.

LEFT The sequence of creation, according to Hindu mythology, culminates in the cosmic man, or Brahma, whose breath creates all living things.

VISHNU IS A BENIGN PRESENCE THAT PERMEATES EVERYTHING (*VISH* MEANS "PERVADE"). HIS CONCERN FOR THE WELFARE OF HUMANITY HAS IN TIMES OF MORAL DECLINE LED HIM TO DESCEND INTO THE WORLD IN VARIOUS FORMS TO RESTORE RIGHTEOUSNESS.

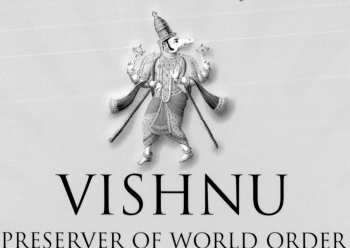

VISHNU
PRESERVER OF WORLD ORDER

ABOVE Vishnu in his third incarnation, as Varaha the Boar.

BACKGROUND Vishnu in his first incarnation, as Matsya the Fish.

Vishnu is believed to have ten incarnations *(avatara)* in the world. Sometimes they have been in the form of giant animals: the Fish, the Turtle, and the Boar. There was also a Man-Lion, and a Dwarf. The most important for worshipers were the seventh and eighth incarnations, which were Rama and Krishna. Krishna has become so popular in India today that he is regarded as a direct manifestation of Vishnu.

As a result of the huge success of Buddhism in India, Vishnu's ninth incarnation was seen by the Brahmins as that of Buddha himself. He took this guise in order to lead wicked men and demons astray by encouraging them to despise the Hindu scriptures, reject the caste system, and deny the existence of gods. In so doing, Buddhists would cause their own annihilation. The final incarnation of Vishnu is set in the future as Kalki, whose task is the redemption of mankind from the evil of the present age.

Vishnu's general representation is as a handsome youth, dark blue in color and dressed like an ancient king. In his four hands he carries a conch shell, a discus, a club, and a lotus flower. His vehicle is the splendid sun bird Garuda, who was the enemy of all serpents.

See also "The Ramayana Epic," page 30.

ABOVE Gods, princes, and other worshipers are blessed by Rama, the seventh incarnation of Vishnu.

BACKGROUND An eighteenth-century southern Indian ivory icon of Vishnu surmounting a throne.

SHIVA, LIKE ALL HINDU DEITIES, IS DEPICTED IN MANY DIFFERENT GUISES AND WITH MANY DIFFERENT ATTRIBUTES. HE IS ALSO KNOWN AS THE DESTROYER, MAHADEVA (THE GREAT GOD), THE SUPREME YOGIN, AND THE LORD OF THE ANIMALS, AND HIS PRIMARY RESPONSIBILITY IS TO MAINTAIN THE CYCLE OF LIFE.

SHIVA
GOD OF THE CYCLE OF LIFE

The third member of the Trimurti, the Hindu trinity, Shiva is a god whose importance has grown over time. His earliest precursor is a seated three-faced figure on seals found in the Indus Valley civilization site of Harappa (third millennium B.C.E.). In the Vedic period (second millennium B.C.E.) he is associated with the storm god, Rudra. But by the time of the *Mahabharata* epic (see page 32) he is portrayed as one of the most powerful of the gods, and sometimes even as the creator of Brahma and Vishnu, the remaining members of the Trimurti.

Shiva is often depicted with three faces, symbolizing his

ABOVE Shiva is the cosmic dancer of creation. He balances destruction, represented by fire, with the rhythm of life. Underfoot he tramples on ignorance, while one leg is raised to symbolize liberation.

three natures—creator, destroyer, and sustainer of the universe. The two outer faces represent the opposites in his nature, including the male and female principles, and the central face is Ishwar, the Supreme One, who transcends all contradictions.

Shiva is an ascetic, symbolized by his matted hair, and the only one of the godhead who is forever in deep meditation. A number of stories tell how various attempts to distract him from his task end in disaster for the tempters. Thus Kama, the Lord of Desires, who tried such a distraction, was consumed by fire when Shiva opened his third eye.

In his role of creator, Shiva is worshiped as the sacred Shiva-linga, the phallus, which is found in all his temples. His consort is the goddess Shakti (a descriptive name for the goddess Devi, meaning "energy"), who symbolizes the divine female.

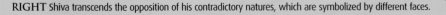

RIGHT Shiva transcends the opposition of his contradictory natures, which are symbolized by different faces.

BACKGROUND Shiva is an ascetic, the only one of the godhead who is forever in deep meditation.

DEVI

THE MOTHER GODDESS

DEVI IS THE GODDESS WITH THE GREATEST POWER IN THE
HINDU PANTHEON. WHATEVER HER GUISE—AND SHE HAS
MANY OF THEM—SHE IS ALWAYS THE WIFE OF THE GOD
SHIVA. BECAUSE HE IS TOO REMOTE TO HAVE DIRECT
CONTACT WITH THE WORLD, DEVI OPERATES AS SHIVA'S
EMANATION. SHE IS THE PERSONIFICATION OF HIS ENERGY
(SHAKTI), A POURING FORTH OF THE CREATIVE LIFE FORCE
THAT MAKES THE WORLD. HER WOMB IS SAID TO HOLD THE
ENTIRE UNIVERSE WITHIN IT.

BACKGROUND In one of her gentler aspects, Devi is the goddess Parvati ("Mountaineer").

Devi is often depicted in art entangled in loving embraces, signifying the eternal process of generation. Her sexual potency made her one of the most worshiped deities in the time of the Tantras, from the seventh century, when devotees found "release" (transition to a blessed realm of consciousness) through the state of being coupled (see "Tantric Yoga," page 82).

The uniting of opposites is symbolized by her dual persona—that of benevolence and ferocity. Gradually over time the different goddesses of different castes in India merged to form the single Great Goddess, who is now worshiped in her many forms. Her gentle aspects include "Light" (Uma), "Mother of the World" (Jaganmata), "the World's Fair One" (Jagadgauri), and "Mountaineer" (Parvati). Her stern side is represented in "the Fierce" (Chandi), "the Black One" (Kali), and "the Terrible" (Bhairavi). Devi is the essential mixture of pleasure and pain, suffering and enlightenment, life and death.

One of her earliest representations in Hindu mythology is as a savior figure, when Vishnu and Shiva found they were unable to combat evil in the world. The gods combined their energies to produce the beautiful warrior-goddess Durga, who, astride a lion, slew the demonic buffalo-monster Mahisha in an epic battle, affirming the triumph of divine power over wickedness.

RIGHT One of the many forms in which Devi is worshiped is as Sarasvati, goddess of education.

47

IN HINDU MYTHOLOGY LAKSHMI IS THE WIFE OF VISHNU AND GODDESS OF BEAUTY, LOVE, AND GOOD FORTUNE. LIKE APHRODITE IN GREEK MYTHOLOGY AND VENUS FOR THE ROMANS, LAKSHMI WAS BORN FROM THE OCEAN—HER NAME MEANS "DAUGHTER OF THE MILK OF THE SEA."

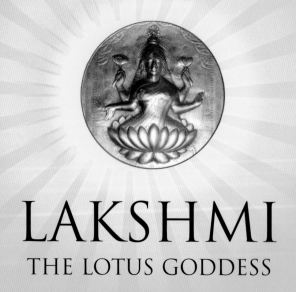

LAKSHMI
THE LOTUS GODDESS

ABOVE Lakshmi's wondrous rising from the ocean, cradled in a golden lotus, symbolizes universal renewal and the beginning of transcendental life.

BACKGROUND
Lakshmi is worshiped as
much for her wisdom as
for her benevolence and
loving nature.

According to one legend, an entanglement of gods and demons were churning the ocean waters when out of the froth rose Lakshmi, in radiant beauty, carrying a lotus in her hand. A lotus is the key symbol for Lakshmi's devotees. It represents the female principle, the womb, procreation and fertility, life-giving waters, divinity, immortality, purity and spiritual strength, and a resting place of the enlightened. A mythical account of Lakshmi describes a thousand-petalled lotus at the heart of each new creation. Lotus-eyed, lotus-colored, and garlanded with lotus flowers, Lakshmi is the epitome of maternal benevolence. Like Devi for her worshipers, Lakshmi is regarded as the universal mother whose ample breasts are a continual source of succor and desire.

In an annual ceremony, ancient Indian rulers went through a ritual of marrying Lakshmi to ensure fertility and good fortune. As consort to Vishnu, she is the vessel of his creative energy, which brings abundant growth in agriculture. In India, good harvests are accompanied by joyous ceremonies of thanksgiving to the Lotus Goddess.

KRISHNA
INCARNATION OF VISHNU

THE MOST WIDELY WORSHIPED GOD IN INDIA IS PRESENTED IN THE *BHAGAVAD GITA* AS THE GOD OF *ALL* THE PEOPLE. IRRESPECTIVE OF THEIR CASTE OR GENDER, WORSHIPERS COULD EMBRACE KRISHNA'S SIMPLE BUT RADICAL MESSAGE THAT THE WAY TO SALVATION IS TO LOVE THE LORD WITH ALL ONE'S HEART, NOT JUST WITH ONE'S MIND OR THROUGH THE PERFECTING OF RITUAL OBSERVANCE.

ABOVE Often depicted as a charming baby, Krishna is hugely popular in Indian worship today.

Indeed, so all-consuming in India was this human icon of love that Krishna came to be identified with God and God with Krishna. Historically, he has assumed several roles that developed independently and then fused sometime in the centuries around the beginning of the common era. There were two main story traditions of Krishna: one as a warrior prince, a divine sage identical in power and wisdom to the god Vishnu himself; the second as a low-caste, frolicsome cowherd who entices local maidens into amorous liaisons by his irresistible flute playing. One maiden in particular, named Radha, is selected and introduced to the full range of love's emotions. It is their love—seen as the perfect deification of daily life— that has become the focus of modern Hindu worship.

Another tradition, popular in the period of medieval Hinduism, depicts Krishna as the Dark One. A myth tells of Vishnu plucking two of his hairs, one black and one white, and implanting them in the wombs of two women. The black hair was born as Krishna,

the white hair as his brother Balarama (also known as Rama). Thus Krishna is portrayed in art as dark haired and dark skinned.

See also "*Bhagavad Gita*" (I) and (II), pages 34–37, and "Hare Krishna," page 120.

BELOW In a nineteenth-century miniature, maidens accompany Krishna's rain-dance at the onset of the rainy season.

AN ELEPHANT-HEADED MAN IS THE GOD OF SUCCESSFUL VENTURES. ENTREPRENEURS AND STUDENTS ENLIST THE AID OF THIS SON OF SHIVA AND PARVATI TO KEEP THEM ON THE PATH OF RIGHTEOUSNESS AND REMOVE ANY OBSTACLES IN THEIR WAY. HIS DEVOTEES MAY BE BLESSED WITH HIS RIGHT HAND AND REWARDED WITH SWEETMEATS IF THEIR ENTERPRISES ARE SUCCESSFUL.

GANESHA
THE ELEPHANT GOD-MAN

ABOVE This Hindu god fulfills the same role played by the classical Greek messenger god, Hermes, and by the Roman messenger god, Mercury.

Ganesha is represented as a short, yellow, potbellied man. He has four hands, and his elephant's head has one tusk, usually broken. Sometimes he is shown riding a rat. He acts as the guardian to his mother's house.

There are several myths accounting for Ganesha's elephant head. One is that Parvati went to have a bath and told her son to guard the door. He did this, even to the extent of preventing his father from entering the chamber. Shiva became so angry that he decapitated Ganesha. Parvati was so upset she threatened to destroy the universe, and so, to pacify her, Shiva promised to replace the head with the first he came upon—which was that of an elephant.

The annual Ganesha festival, held after the monsoon rains around the end of August, commemorates the birth of the elephant god. Shiva is said to have refused to conceive a son with Parvati, so she manufactured one by scrubbing flesh from her body and molding it into human form before commanding it to life. The festival is celebrated particularly enthusiastically in western India. Participants may make an image of Ganesha out of clay and keep it in their homes for ten days before forming a procession to carry the images down to a nearby river or well, where they are immersed ritually. Devotional songs and folk dances are also performed.

ABOVE The dancing Ganesha, with the body of a man and head of an elephant, has no fear of death.

BACKGROUND Ganesha is worshiped in many temples in the Deccan in central India.

HANUMAN
THE MONKEY GOD

THE STRENGTH AND VERSATILITY OF DIVINE POWER IS EMBODIED IN HANUMAN, A DEXTEROUS MONKEY GOD. HANUMAN'S ABILITY TO CHANGE HIS SHAPE AND SIZE AT WILL, AS WELL AS TO LEAP GREAT DISTANCES THROUGH THE AIR, PROVIDES A SPECTACULAR ELEMENT IN EASTERN MYTHOLOGY, NOTABLY IN THE INDIAN EPIC *RAMAYANA*, IN WHICH HE FIGURES AS THE ARMY GENERAL AND CHIEF ADVISER TO THE MONKEY KING.

ABOVE Hanuman holds aloft the goal of his mission: to free Sita, Rama's wife.

OPPOSITE The triumphant Hanuman returns, mission completed.

An Indian poet, talking about Hanuman, describes how his form is as vast as a mountain and as tall as a colossal tower, whenever he chooses. His complexion is yellow and glowing like molten gold, a marvelous sight when he dashes from place to place; his enormous tail is so long that the end is hard to find. He roars like thunder, flies among the clouds with a rushing noise, and disturbs the surface of the ocean as he speeds by.

His special characteristics are well illustrated in the *Ramayana* (see page 30) when he comes to the aid of Rama, whose wife has been abducted. The monkey god uses his wily detective instinct to follow her trail and discovers she is being held captive on the island of Sri Lanka. In the ensuing combat, a female demon tries to swallow him whole, but he distends his body, forcing her mouth to open enormously. Then he shrinks to the size of a thumb, rushes through her head, and escapes via her right ear.

Joining forces with Rama, Hanuman and his army of monkeys fight with clubs and defeat the captors of Rama's wife, sacking the enemy capital. For his courage and services "special agent" Hanuman is rewarded with the gift of eternal life and youth.

ONE OF THE MOST IMPORTANT BELIEFS HELD BY
WORSHIPERS OF VISHNU (THE "PRESERVER") IS THAT THE
DEITY DESCENDS TO EARTH AT TIMES OF CRISIS AND IS
BORN IN CREATURELY FORM TO PROTECT THE WORLD FROM
EVIL FORCES. VAISHNAVIS (DEVOTEES OF VISHNU) HAVE A
RELATIVELY HIGH APPRECIATION OF THE VALUE OF
WORLDLY LIFE AND BELIEVE IN A KINDLY GOD WHO IS
CONCERNED FOR THE WELFARE OF THE WORLD.

AVATARS
INCARNATIONS OF THE DIVINE

The term *avatar* usually refers to Vishnu's ten appearances: as Fish (Matsya), Turtle (Kurma), Boar (Varaha), Man-lion (Narasimha), Dwarf (Vamana), Rama with an ax (Parasurama), Rama as hero of the *Ramayana* epic, Krishna, Buddha, and Kalki, the avatar yet to come. Although all the figures feature in myths recounting Vishnu's activity in the world, only the ninth avatar, Buddha, is with certainty a historical person.

Parasurama, Rama, and Krishna may have been real people who fought for independence against evil overlords.

Some of the myths are explanations of how the world came to be as it is. Incarnated as the Boar, for example, Vishnu plunged into the ocean and, with his snout, raised the drowning world, which lay submerged on the bottom after being dumped there by a demon. As the Fish, Vishnu warned Manu (the equivalent of Noah in

RIGHT The fourth avatar, Narasimha the Man-lion, fought a titanic struggle to re-assert the authority of Vishnu. A protracted duel ended with Narasimha tearing his enemy apart.

Judeo-Christian tradition) that a universal flood was coming, and pulled the boat he built to safety.

Although most Hindus recognize ten avatars, some traditions believe there are more—the number varying according to local preference. Some modern reform movements, such as the Arya Samaj (Aryan Society), have rejected the entire list of avatars as superstitious. Other schools of thought have broadened the concept to include any holy person. Saints *(sadhus)*, both dead and alive, are often thought to be incarnations

of a deity and may even include figures from other religions. Some Hindus, for example, believe that Jesus Christ is an avatar of Vishnu.

Some devotional movements center themselves on avatar figures for the purpose of drawing on their divinity and gaining psychic power *(siddhi)*. In turn, adherents may manifest such aspects of the paranormal as levitation and bilocation.

See also "Vishnu," page 42.

DEVAS
THE VEDIC GODS

THE ARYANS WHO SETTLED IN INDIA IN ABOUT 1500 B.C.E.
WERE PASTORALISTS WHO WORSHIPED NATURAL
PHENOMENA. THE PRESENCE OF THEIR GODS WAS SEEN IN
ALL ASPECTS OF NATURE, SUCH AS THE WIND, RAIN,
THUNDER, OCEAN, AND SUN.

ABOVE Agni, god of fire, was a key deity in ancient India—the maker of the sun and stars.

OPPOSITE A tenth-century relief panel depicts a series of Vedic goddesses, who personify in various ways the
attributes of their male partners, including a bull, peacock, boar, and serpents.

Their chief deity was Indra, a god of storm and conquest, whose weapon was the thunderbolt. The character of Indra in the *Rig Veda* is portrayed as a great fighter, a slayer of demons, and a lusty drinker of the beverage prepared by the ritual god Soma. Probably a hallucinogen of some kind, the drink called *soma* and its exhilarating qualities seem to have been appreciated by the gods and their priests, the Brahmins.

Another important deity was Agni, the god of fire and sacrifice. The hymns addressed to him clearly were composed by poets intoxicated with soma. Quite possibly the growing interest in yoga after 900 B.C.E. was prompted by a yearning to recapture this ecstasy, which had been lost when the Aryans moved out of the mountains where the plant grew.

Perhaps the most distinguished deity in Vedic mythology was Varuna, god of the cosmic order, who embodied the sky. As the ancient wisdom underlying Hinduism, he was guardian of the divine principle of order, known as rita. He created the sun, hollowed out channels for the rivers, and saw that the ocean was never too full. Through his commands the moon kept its course and the stars remained in the firmament. Having unlimited power, Varuna controlled the destiny of humankind, sustaining life and offering protection from evil. Those who did not speak the truth became the objects of his wrath, yet he had a reputation for gentleness and a tendency to forgive. He could also confer immortality, which he guarded carefully together with Yama, the god of death.

CHAPTER 4

the QUEST FOR salvation

The Hindu's ultimate goal is to attain moksha, that is, personal liberation from the cycle of birth, death, and rebirth, known as samsara. This can be achieved through dharma, the sacred code of conduct both ritual (prayers, worship) and moral.

Hindus recognize a number of traditional paths leading to liberation: of devotion, action, and knowledge. Devotion (bhakti) is the simplest way of experiencing the union that exists between the individual soul (atman) and the universal spirit (Brahman, or God). The path of action (karma) requires Hindus to think and behave selflessly, so that the consequent effects, both good and evil, do not bind the atman to successive lives in different bodies. The path of knowledge (jnana) must be learned from a guru who can explain from the sacred scriptures the nature of Brahman, atman, the universe, and our place in it.

ACCORDING to HINDU BELIEF, BRAHMAN IS THE ONE GOD, OR UNIVERSAL SPIRIT DESCRIBED IN THE UPANISHAD SCRIPTURES. IT IS THE PRIMAL ESSENCE WITH WHICH EVERY HINDU STRIVES TO UNITE HIS OR HER SOUL (THE atman) BY TRANSCENDING THE NORMAL CARES OF WORLDLY EXISTENCE.

BRAHMAN
AND ATMAN
THE ESSENCES OF GOD
AND MANKIND

The ultimate goal for the Hindu is to merge his or her self, or soul (atman), into the great spirit of the universe (Brahman). A certain union of the two already exists, inasmuch as they are of the same essence, but they are kept apart by worldly influences. When these influences are reduced sufficiently, it is possible for an individual to experience the union with Brahman.

Both concepts have evolved since Vedic times when Brahman was believed to be a mysterious power invoked during the recitation of sacred hymns to affect the natural world. By the time of the Upanishads (c. 200 B.C.E.), Brahman was thought of as the latent power in all things, and was further refined as the mysterious and unknowable "consciousness" that creates and maintains the world of being. Similar thinking lay behind the understanding of atman, which is like the "root of a tree of life,"* the vital principle that sustains life. Though the two concepts are the same in essence, a distinction can be drawn between them. For example, atman is the source of bliss, which we may experience, whereas Brahman is bliss itself; atman is mankind's being in the world, but Brahman is being itself.

In representing the intrinsic human self, atman is a deeper entity within ourselves than the ego or personality. Ascetics attempt to reach this core of being by stripping away the "layers" that cover the self like clothes. These layers include the physical body, the subtle body of the *chakras* (see "Subtle Energy," page 70) and our causal body (consisting of the sum of our karma). Deeper still lie the psychic organs, sense faculties that explore the outer world and report to the inner faculties of the psyche. Herein lies the *buddhi* (intellect), the means of thinking and making decisions, which is also the seat of our consciousness, which in turn originates from atman.

In reaching one's atman, one is accessing the knowledge of all truth through Brahman. And, by knowing Brahman, one becomes Brahman.

*R. E. Hume (trans. and ed.), *The Thirteen Principal Upanishads*, New York: OUP, 1962.

ABOVE Brahman, the universal soul, has different aspects to reflect continuity and change. Brahma, the creator aspect, has four faces to symbolize four epochs of time, and four arms for the four quarters of the universe.

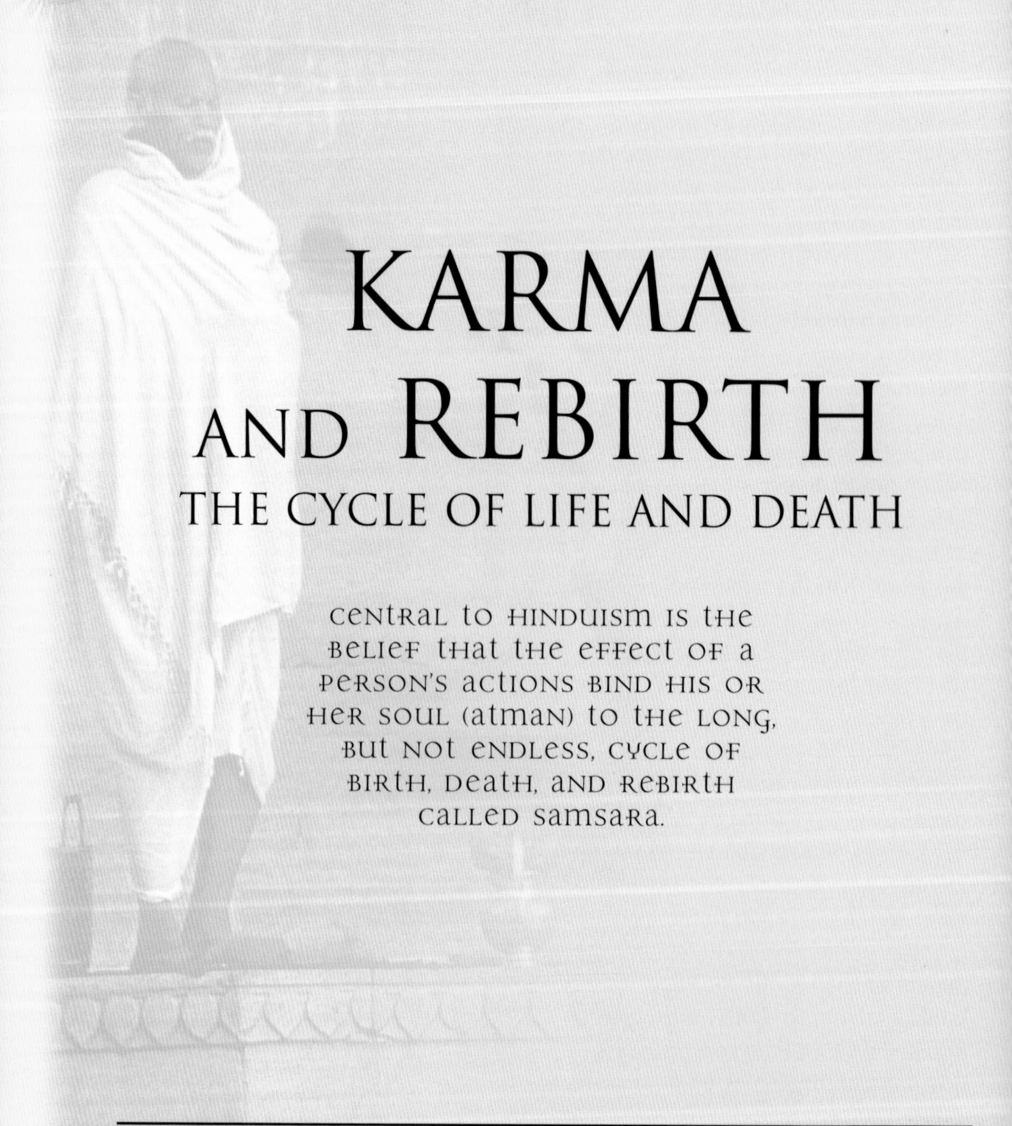

KARMA
AND REBIRTH
THE CYCLE OF LIFE AND DEATH

CENTRAL TO HINDUISM IS THE
BELIEF THAT THE EFFECT OF A
PERSON'S ACTIONS BIND HIS OR
HER SOUL (atman) TO THE LONG,
BUT NOT ENDLESS, CYCLE OF
BIRTH, DEATH, AND REBIRTH
CALLED SAMSARA.

BACKGROUND Pilgrims come to the sacred waters of the Ganges to cleanse their spirits and help liberate their souls from the continuous cycle of birth and rebirth.

64

Deeds, good and bad, committed during a lifetime carry a kind of spiritual charge that is borne by the soul to its future incarnation, a process called karma. The balance between merit and sin in a life determines how a person will be born in the future, whether as an animal or a human, and, if as a human, with what status.

Karma basically means "action," but it also means the invisible energy thought to be generated by the performance of all activities, both physical and mental. Long after the act or thought has been committed, its energy continues to exist unobserved, some think external to the body, others believe internally, psychologically.

The accumulation of karma gives benefits, such as good health, good looks, intelligence, and longevity. In wrongdoers it produces the opposite effects.

Allied to the concepts of karma and rebirth is the caste system. Though individuals cannot escape the caste into which they are born, they may move to a different caste for their future lives. As a result, Hindus understand themselves to have a long history of good and evil deeds committed in former lives, and that each person's current situation justly reflects the stage of his or her soul's journey. Hence every Hindu accepts his or her "station" in life.

Every soul, over a number of lives, can achieve the goal of liberation (moksha) by breaking the cycle of samsara through performing dutiful, selfless actions. In this way karma can be seen as a positive force, rather than the fatalistic concept it often appears to be.

ABOVE The Hindu symbol of creation shows Brahma having emerged from the navel of Vishnu.

HINDUS BELIEVE THAT THE UNIVERSE IS A COMPLEX BUT
ESSENTIALLY UNCHANGING ORDER AND THAT EVERY ENTITY
WITHIN IT MUST BEHAVE ACCORDING TO THE LAWS
PRESCRIBED FOR ITS OWN PARTICULAR NATURE. THIS
NATURAL LAW IS KNOWN AS DHARMA, AND AT THE HUMAN
LEVEL IT IS THE SOURCE OF MORAL LAW.

DHARMA
RIGHT LIVING

The root meaning of *dharma* is "to make firm" or "to preserve," and indicates a world that is firmly structured. The world changes seasonally, but its order on a grand scale is self-perpetuating, a finely tuned eco-balance that demands of all its participants an obedience to the universal laws that have been revealed in the Hindu scriptures. For mankind, this means following a pattern of ideal behavior, with moral, social, and ritual obligations.

Even within these categories of obligation there is a distinction between a general code of ethics applicable to everyone, such as being honest, not causing injury, and offering charity, and duties that pertain to one's particular caste. Within one's caste one must behave according to the stage of life one has reached (see "Stages

---

OPPOSITE LEFT Many Hindus possess images of deities, called *murtis*, which like the image pictured here show aspects of the gods to symbolize their power.

of Life," page 96). Rather than commanding a general edict for all, dharma determines custom-made sets of rules for each individual.

To fulfill one's dharmic duty is to live true to one's rightful place within the universe. In doing so, an individual demonstrates devotion to God, as well as satisfying his or her own spiritual needs. Failure to keep to the right path may generate bad karma and jeopardize the long-term progress of the soul. As a verse of the *Bhagavad Gita* says:

> Better one's own duty, poorly done,
> Than the duty of another,
>   well-performed.
> Doing the work natural to one's self,
> One incurs no guilt.
>   (18:47)

See also "Karma and Rebirth," page 64.

ABOVE RIGHT The source of the sacred River Ganges, in the foothills of the Himalayas, is one of the holiest sites in Hinduism and is often visited by those who have reached the ascetic stage of life.

VEDANTA PHILOSOPHY

GOD AND SOUL

PHILOSOPHY AND RELIGION ARE CLOSELY INTERTWINED IN HINDU TRADITION, AND HINDU THINKERS THROUGH THE AGES HAVE PRODUCED THE SUBTLEST OF SPECULATIONS ON THE NATURE OF REALITY. THE MOST IMPORTANT SCHOOL OF THOUGHT WAS KNOWN AS VEDANTA (MEANING "END OF THE VEDAS"), WHICH DERIVED FROM THE UPANISHADS.

ABOVE Much of Hindu thought is expressed in mythical terms, including Nandi, the bull that carries Shiva and protects all four-legged creatures.

The central theme of the Vedanta was "monism"— namely that there is only one indivisible reality (Brahman, or God) and that the soul (atman) is one with it. This philosophy was later developed by three important schools based on the interpretations of their founders, Shankara, Ramanuja, and Madhva. The first of these, Shankara, was a philosopher, mystic, and poet, who according to tradition was born in 788 and lived only thirty-two years. His saintliness was such that he was regarded as an incarnation of Shiva.

Shankara's teachings formed the Advaita, or "nondualism," school, that is the belief that the soul and God are of one substance, which many Hindus still maintain today. Shankara argued that only Brahman was real; everything else, including all the visible world and even one's sense of individuality, is unreal. It appeared to be real only because of Brahman's power of illusion (maya). Once an individual realizes this fact, through yoga and enlightenment, his or her soul merges with Brahman.

In contrast to Shankara, Ramanuja in the twelfth century taught that the everyday world is not an illusion. And the atman, although a fragment of Brahman, is not identical with it. The soul retains its individuality and exists in an eternal relationship with God. The best way to liberate the soul, so that it can reunite with God, is through bhakti, or love of God.

Yet another view was put forward in the thirteenth century by Madhva, who taught a system of "dualism," stating that Brahman was distinct from atman. They remain separate from each other, not only in the created world but even after the atman has achieved liberation.

ABOVE Brahma, god of creation, himself was born in a womb-like substance, maya, which according to Hindu belief hides the world from true reality in Brahman.

IN HINDU TRADITION, THE ATMAN, OR IMMORTAL TRUE SELF, IS SURROUNDED BY THREE BODIES. ONLY ONE OF THESE—THE STHULA SHARIRA, OR MORTAL BODY OF FLESH AND BONE—IS VISIBLE TO THE HUMAN EYE. THE OTHER TWO ARE IMMORTAL— THE SUKSMA SHARIRA, THE SUBTLE OR ASTRAL BODY, AND THE KARANA SHARIRA, THE BODY THAT DETERMINES WHAT YOUR NEXT INCARNATION WILL BE.

SUBTLE ENERGY
THE INVISIBLE BODY

The Suksma Sharira is composed of seven chakras, or energy centers, and the *nadis*, the channels through which the *prana* (vital force; see "Hatha Yoga," page 76) flows to regulate the body's functions. There are said to be 72,000 main nadis, and many more secondary nadis. The principal nadi is the Sushumna, which rises from the base of the spine to the top of the head, passing through the seven chakras.

The chakras (the word means "wheels") are energy centers spaced along the Sushumna nadi at the points in the astral body where the nadis meet. Each chakra is associated with a color, geometrical shape, number of lotus petals, and *mantra* (sound). Although there is no physical evidence for the existence of the seven chakras, some authorities claim that there is a degree of concordance between their location in the astral body and the major nerves and glands in the physical body. When practicing visualization techniques, yogis consciously direct the flow of prana to the chakras. The lower chakras are concerned with the physical plane of existence, while the higher chakras are thought to be gateways to the higher realms of the spirit.

BELOW The seven chakras and their bodily location, from the top down: Sahasrara chakra, crown; Ajna chakra, third eye; Vishuddha chakra, throat; Anahata chakra, heart; Manipura chakra, solar plexus; Swadhishtana chakra, pelvis; Muladhara chakra, root.

YOGA

ORIGINS AND FORMS

YOGA IS A SET OF PSYCHOSOMATIC TECHNIQUES FOR
PRACTICING MEDITATION, AND IT COMES IN DIFFERENT
FORMS. SOME METHODS FOCUS ON PHYSICAL EXERCISES,
WHEREAS OTHERS PLACE GREATER EMPHASIS ON
SPIRITUAL AWARENESS.

Each method of yoga teaches a particular "path" based on a certain set of beliefs and practices. Some are more demanding than others, and all the types of yoga together constitute a sort of ladder of spiritual attainment, from the "lowest" form of Hatha yoga, with its concentration on posture and breathing, to the "highest" form, known as Raja, or classical, yoga.

Yoga is unique to South Asia and has its roots in the distant past. It is not possible to be precise about a time or place of origin. A clay figurine of a man in a lotus position was found at an archaeological site of the ancient Indus Valley civilization (c. 2000 B.C.E.). The Vedas scriptures (completed c. 800 B.C.E.) describe body postures and breathing exercises, as well as the attainment of paranormal capabilities. But yoga in its classic form—the "eight-limbed"

system of meditation, from which most of today's practices stem—was not compiled until c. 300–500 by Patanjali, in the *Yoga Sutra* (see "Raja Yoga," page 74).

What Patanjali and later refiners of his model presented was a sophisticated theoretical method for transforming human awareness. A belief in the existence of a supreme personal being, a lord (Isvara), underlies classical yoga, though it is more symbolic than actual, and serves as a meditative device for the yogi. A variety of auxiliary techniques, including visual and auditory symbols, and ritual activities have also developed. To these categories belong the types of yoga called Mantra, Tantric, Laya, and Kundalini. In recent years, further developments include Power yoga and Iyengar Hatha, as well as numerous variations on themes taught by different instructors.

OPPOSITE In the West the focus in yoga is on the physical side, but its true purpose is spiritual development.

BACKGROUND The lotus position is the classic poise for yoga, as shown here by the Buddha.

Often called the "royal road" because of its directness, Raja yoga is the classical form of yoga exercise for turning our mental and physical energies into spiritual energy, mainly through meditation. In aiming to still the mind, the yogi hopes to experience different levels of awareness.

RAJA YOGA
CLASSICAL YOGA

Meditation cannot begin until the body and its energy are in balance. Various means of relaxation are employed to achieve this state. Then the yogi will begin what is known as the eight-limbed meditation, which leads to absolute mental control and concentration. The first five of these "limbs" are external or preparatory, the last three internal.

The first five "limbs" are interpersonal restraint (such as not injuring or lying to your fellow human beings); internal restraint (including personal hygiene, good moral values); physical fitness so that bodily postures conducive to good meditation can be sustained; cultivation of an awareness of the respiratory processes and control over them; and the capacity to detach one's sense capacities (such as sight and hearing) from their objects. The sixth "limb" is sustained concentration on a single object of meditation; the seventh is attaining an even flow of awareness in relation to that object; and the eighth is the attainment of a trancelike awareness in meditation, in which the distinction between oneself and the object of meditation disappears. In this condition one can experience the inherent nature of awareness, and begin to distinguish between ordinary awareness and pure consciousness, which is the essence of ultimate unchanging reality, the Hindu understanding of God. The practitioner of Raja yoga concentrates on one point in order to integrate all diffused attention. By so doing, the yogi can eventually hold his or her attention steady, and close off all distractions. Daydreaming, floating thoughts, or impulses must not be allowed to dominate the mind.

ABOVE The ancient discipline of yoga exercise is now popular in the West.

LEFT An eighteenth-century miniature painting shows an Indian yogi in practice.

THE MOST POPULAR FORM OF YOGA IN THE WEST IS ALSO THE MOST BASIC. HATHA IS DESCRIBED IN THE UPANISHADS AS A RIGOROUS PROGRAM OF BODILY DISCIPLINE, INVOLVING UNCOMFORTABLE POSTURES, BREATHING EXERCISES, AND DIET CONTROL.

HATHA YOGA
YOGA OF VITALITY

Hatha is generally used by yogis as a preparation for higher forms of meditation, such as Raja yoga. Some eighty different body postures *(asanas)* are enumerated, including the famous lotus position of sitting cross-legged with an upright back and open palms. Complex breathing exercises are prescribed with specific measures of time to inhale, retain breath, and exhale. Together with dietary constraints, the purpose of these exercises is to cleanse the blood arteries and channels of the body, and to reactivate blocked sources of creative energy (shakti) that lie within the chakras (the seven centers of spiritual energy).

The word *Hatha* is an amalgam of "sun" *(ha)* and "moon" *(tha)*, and symbolizes the positive (sun) and negative (moon) currents in the body. The balancing of the two is seen as the means to harmonizing and mastering these currents so that "vital force" (prana) can be controlled. In so doing, the mind will be cleared and the path open to experiencing higher states of consciousness.

People in the West have found Hatha yoga useful for different

purposes. Busy executives practice it to control their stress levels; pregnant women use it in preparation for giving birth; athletes use it to help themselves focus on achieving high levels of performance. Depending on one's requirements, Hatha yoga can be adapted accordingly. The vigorous approach developed by B. K. S. Iyengar in India has helped many people benefit from this method. Iyengar emphasizes the need to build strength, stamina, and correct body alignment to attain better concentration and relaxation. By encouraging weak parts to strengthen and stiff areas to stretch, the body can be brought into alignment. A well-balanced body will move more freely, require less muscular work, and be able to relax more naturally.

ABOVE A yogi master is attended by his servant in an eighteenth-century painting.

LEFT Yoga demands a tremendous effort of balanced control over the body.

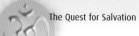

LAYA YOGA
YOGA OF DISSOLUTION

The aim of Laya Yoga is total absorption into the divine through concentration on the chakras (spiritual energy centers). The process can be conducted by various means.

ABOVE By concentrating on the heart chakra, symbolized by twelve golden petals, a yogi can open "doors" to higher levels of consciousness and feelings of unconditional love.

There are five main chakras in the spine and two in the head. Under the guidance of a yoga guru, the Laya yoga practitioner learns how to find these centers mentally, and in so doing opens "doorways" to different realms of higher consciousness. For example, the heart chakra lies within the spine behind the heart. By activating this chakra through meditation, the yogi will expand his or her consciousness and see in the mind's eye a great expanse of blue (and sometimes other colors). In the process, a strong sense of love is felt, helping him or her to overcome fears, anxieties, and self-centeredness.

Another method of Laya yoga is to find the source of an inner, mystical sound, thought to be a manifestation of primal matter. To do this the practitioner focuses on the lower of the two head chakras, which lies between the eyebrows. It is known in Hinduism as the third eye. With the eyeballs rolled upward beneath closed lids, the yogi listens for a sound in the right ear. The sound may vary from one person to another, but is contained internally and cannot be heard by anyone else. With concentration on the sound, the yogi becomes oblivious to external things, overcomes all distractions, and loses consciousness of the personal self. By mentally "entering" the sound, the yogi reaches the stage of absorption into a higher realm of consciousness. He or she will experience a blissful state and is said to become endowed with spiritual powers capable of producing visions and paranormal phenomena.

ABOVE The sixth chakra, located between the eyebrows and known in Hinduism as the "third eye," is thought to endow a practitioner of Laya with the psychic power of clairvoyance.

MANTRA YOGA, MEANING "UNION BY VOICE OR SOUND," IS
THE PRACTICE OF UTTERING SACRED SOUNDS IN RHYTHMIC
REPETITION. CERTAIN SYLLABLES, WHICH DERIVE FROM THE
SANSKRIT ALPHABET, ARE BELIEVED TO HAVE THE POWER TO
CREATE ALTERED STATES OF CONSCIOUSNESS,
AND PERHAPS TO HEAL.

MANTRA YOGA

YOGA OF SOUND

A chant, or mantra, is a single word or sound repeated continually by the practitioner for weeks and months, sometimes for even more than a year. It is often used as a tool to help focus the mind on a single thought until the mind is free from all other intrusive thoughts and is still. It is believed that the power of a mantra lies in its vibrational charge. Physicists say that all matter consists of electrons and protons coexisting in a state of vibrational interplay. Mantra yoga endeavors to tune in to certain patterns of universal vibration through utterance. It is, therefore, crucial that the word, or sound, be uttered with the correct pronunciation and intonement. All of the key sounds in world religions—*Om*, *Aum* (both Hindu), *Amin* (Muslim), *Amen* (Christian)—are derived from Om, which Hindus regard as the original vibration in the universe and the master mantra on which all other mantras are based. The formulation of mantras is so precise that they can be designed to awaken certain chakras

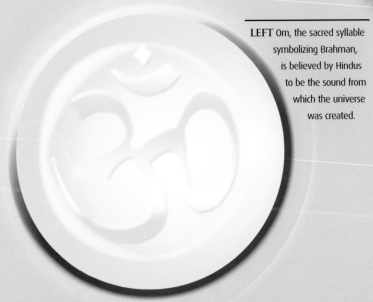

(centers of spiritual energy) in the
body. Known as *bija* mantras, they
operate like keys to the seven chakras.
In ascending order they are *Lam, Vam,
Ram, Yam, Ham, Ksam*, and *Bam*
(or *Om*).

Not all mantras need to be uttered
out loud. There are three forms: oral,
semi-oral, and silent. Oral repetition,
which is audible to anyone, is usually
considered the lowest form, and silent
repetition the highest. Some Hindus,
such as the Krishna sect, believe that
oral chanting is more powerful. The
semi-oral form involves vibrating the
vocal cords but emitting no sound.
Traditionally Hindus believe that when
the mantra is practiced correctly, the
vibrations created are so strong that
everything in the universe is touched
by them. It is thought that yogis can
use their mantric power creatively as
well as destructively, and can perform
psychokinetic feats, such as levitation,
apports (the transporting of material
objects by the power of the mind), and
even the emission of vibrations to
influence the weather.

Tantric yoga is an unusual discipline. Whereas orthodox Hindu meditation strives to renounce the senses in an ascetic mode, the Tantric variety aims to harness sexual energy as a means to enlightenment. Its practitioners say sexuality contains enormous power, which, if released in a controlled way, can induce a state of blissful oneness with the divine.

TANTRIC YOGA

YOGA OF SEX

antrism in India has long had a suspect, peripheral image. It is often associated with dubious practices of the occult, and orthodox Hinduism tends to distance itself from it. However, Tantrists claim their practice brings authentic divine experience. In agreement with the rest of Hinduism, they conceive of Brahman (the ultimate reality, or God) as a union of the male and female principles, namely Shiva and Shakti. In Hindu mythology, the universe arose as a result of their copulation. Shiva represents the cosmic principles of cognition, wisdom, and quiescence, whereas Shakti is creative energy and action. In striving to return to a state of oneness with ultimate reality, Tantric yoga reverses, as it were, the process of creation. Through sexual union, the man, who identifies with Shiva, and the woman, who identifies with Shakti, transcend this cosmic duality to merge with the Absolute.

In the traditional form of this yoga, a "circle" of participants begin their ritual by chanting Vedic and Tantric hymns. Each person then silently meditates on his or her special mantra given by a presiding guru, and at the same time imbibes large quantities of an aphrodisiac drink, made up of marijuana, sherbet, and sweet milk. In a suitable state of arousal, the participants pair off. The Shaktis sit astride their Shivas and begin copulating, in line with the doctrinal idea of woman as energy and man as quiescence.

The aim of Tantric practice is to awaken a dormant power, known as *kundalini*, which is thought to reside at the base of the spine. To do this, it is crucial for the male to avoid ejaculation. In an act of simultaneous control of the mind, breath, and semen, kundalini is rushed up the spine to the topmost chakra of the Subtle Body (see "Subtle Energy," page 70), and a wonderful state of bliss results. This experience is identified with the merger of Shiva and Shakti in a reenactment of cosmic union. The emphasis of Tantrism, therefore, is not on sexual release, but on the use of sex as a channel by which the Self may be realized.

See also "Kundalini Yoga," page 90.

LEFT Shiva as the hermaphrodite, representing union between the male and female principles.

BACKGROUND Most erotic imagery on Hindu shrines is inspired by Tantrism.

तपकरञ्रासन ३२

JNANA YOGA
YOGA OF KNOWLEDGE

IN THE CONTEXT OF JNANA YOGA, KNOWLEDGE MEANS NOT
COLLECTED INFORMATION BUT RATHER AN UNDERSTANDING
OF THE NATURE OF CONSCIOUSNESS. THIS KNOWLEDGE
COMES ONLY TO THOSE WHO, THROUGH EXPERIENCE AND
PERSISTENT EXAMINATION, LEARN TO PERCEIVE THE SUBTLE
DISTINCTION BETWEEN THE UNCHANGING SELF, OR PURE
CONSCIOUSNESS (*PURUSA*), AND ORDINARY AWARENESS IN
ONE'S EMBODIED CONDITION (*CITTA*).

The strenuous demands of this discipline, which are outlined in the *Bhagavad Gita*, make this type of yoga one of the hardest to practice, and it is normally undertaken only after integrating the lessons of other, simpler yoga disciplines. The aim is to use the mind to investigate its own nature, through reflective meditation, and to transcend its limitations. As an analogy, we may perceive the space inside and outside a glass beaker as different, just as we see ourselves as separate from God. By exercising Jnana yoga we strive to break the glass and dissolve our separation from God.

The tradition of Jnana yoga teaches that liberation (moksha) is achieved not by works or ritual but by knowledge alone. Since knowledge can be attained from either revealed scripture or from mystical experience, yogis who choose the Jnana path may combine the two. They can study the findings of the great seers, and then assess them in the light of their own experience.

LEFT Jnana yoga may include some of the most extreme forms of ascetic practice.

BACKGROUND Through reflective meditation, sadhus (holy men) use their minds to attempt to transcend the normal bounds of consciousness.

KARMA YOGA
YOGA OF ACTION

Karma Yoga is the consecration of all actions to
God. Its practice is so-called because it aims to
negate karma—the good and bad spiritual
consequences of our actions.

ABOVE Karma Yoga is exacting in its discipline of movements.

The word karma means not only action but the result of the action—the effect on our spirit. There are three kinds of karma: good, bad, and mixed. Good karma turns us into God; bad karma sends us into the wombs of animals; mixed actions give us human rebirth. According to Hindu thinking, all actions are relative. There is no absolute good work or bad work in this world. Every bad action has a redeeming factor, however minute, and every good work bears an element of evil (such as an underlying motive like selfishness or pride).

Vitally important in the practice of Karma yoga is detachment from the fruits of one's actions. We must expect no reward, no outcome from our actions; then we will accrue no karma and attain liberation. Karma binds us to the cycle of repeated existences when actions are performed with selfish motives. We have to consider ourselves as operating as an instrument in the hands of God, with perfectly negated desires and expectations. Such practitioners of this type of yoga will have no fear (of consequences), nor will they suffer sorrow; instead, they should rejoice in suffering.

Furthermore, by endeavoring to live a selfless life, one ensures that the heart grows pure and the yogi will discern more easily right from wrong. By thinking, speaking, and acting in a right way, people can alter their habits and improve their character. Ultimately, they will determine their own destiny. If people understand this law of karma correctly, they may scale the heights of sublime spirituality and be able to bear the burden of samsara with patience, endurance, and strength of mind.

RIGHT Hindu ashrams, like this one at Rishikesh, are meeting places for religious communities and often also provide shelter for pilgrims.

THE APPROACH TO BECOMING ONE WITH GOD THROUGH
BHAKTI YOGA IS MOTIVATED BY THE POWER OF LOVE. GOD IS
SEEN AS THE EMBODIMENT OF LOVE, AND BY WHATEVER
MEANS THEY FIND MOST PERSONALLY SUITABLE, DEVOTEES
CHANNEL THEIR EMOTIONS INTO UNCONDITIONAL LOVE OF
GOD. ACCORDING TO PROFESSOR JOHN HINNELLS, "IT IS
BHAKTI THAT HAS INSPIRED THE GREATER PART OF
HINDUISM TO THE PRESENT DAY."*

BHAKTI YOGA
THE YOGA OF LOVE

In some ways, the Bhakti path is the easiest of the yoga disciplines. Bhakti is a natural expression of human inclinations. Without frustrating human instincts, it gradually brings the individual to union with the divine through a progressive realization of God. To begin with, the devotee must endeavor to perform all his or her daily acts with God in mind: Before eating, the food must be offered to God, for its purification; if walking in a garden, the flowers should be offered to God; when browsing in a market, the merchandise should likewise be offered to God. In this way, just as flowers grow in a garden, so one's love for God will grow in the heart.

There is, therefore, no specific method in Bhakti, only an attitude of mind and heart. By training one's mind and will, one can develop an intuitive realization of God. Ordinary forms of idol worship in temples and at home

---

* John R. Hinnells (ed.), *A Handbook of Living Religions,* London: Viking, 1984.

serve as simple inductions into Bhakti. Hindu scriptures recommend devotion to God by various means. Singing and chanting, hearing recitations of divine stories, and the mere enunciation of God's name—all are ways to merge the mind with the divine. Added to this is service to others, especially the poor and the sick, for the ultimate aim is to surrender the self to the love of God. By channeling one's energies and emotions to whatever is other than oneself, one softens the heart and removes the selfish instincts of jealousy, anger, pride, lust, and arrogance—all aspects of the ego that bind one to the samsaric wheel, the cycle of birth, death, and rebirth. It is in daily life that Bhakti yoga is truly practiced. In the Christian tradition, Jesus exemplified its ideal when he taught, "As you have loved me, love one another."

ABOVE Bhakti yoga has no prescribed method. Its simple idea of giving oneself to God involves serving others to make them happy.

KUNDALINI YOGA

SERPENT POWER

THE POWER OF KUNDALINI, a PSYCHOSPIRITUAL ENERGY
DORMANT IN THE BODY, IS SAID TO BE HUGE AND CAPABLE
OF BRINGING NEW LEVELS OF CONSCIOUSNESS, INCLUDING
MYSTICAL INSIGHT AND PHYSICAL AWARENESS.

P art of the "Subtle Body," the dormant energy of kundalini can be roused during meditation. Kundalini has been dubbed "liquid fire" or "liquid light" by those who have experienced its more sensational effects. However, the yogi, who wishes to liberate his or her self from the senses, must ignore the generation of these occult powers (siddhi) if he or she is to achieve redemption. In this yoga, the yogi meditates to arouse kundalini (which means "serpent power" in Sanskrit, because it is said to lie coiled like a serpent in the root chakra at the base of the spine). Like a snake, the power is summoned to rise through the body. First the yogi will feel heat at the base of the spine, then the energy will move up a psychic channel parallel to the spinal column. As it rises, kundalini activates each of the chakras.

The lower parts of the body turn cold as kundalini rises toward the brain. In the process, which might last a few minutes or happen like a thunderbolt, the yogi may shake, perhaps violently, feel pain, turn hot and cold, hear mysterious sounds, and see illuminations. The aim is to raise the energy to the crown chakra, where it unites with Shiva. The yogi will try to prevent the energy from falling to chakras below the heart, since to do so is thought to inflate the ego and arouse strong sexual desire. By mastering the flow of kundalini, the yogi may succeed in bringing the energy to lodge permanently in the crown chakra.

Yogis emphasize that the body must be properly prepared before any attempt is made to practice Kundalini yoga, since there are inherent dangers in tapping its powerful energy.

See also "Tantric Yoga," page 82.

LEFT The source of the potent kundalini energy lies at the base of the spine in the root chakra, the lowest of the seven spiritual centers of the body and the seat of our animal nature.

CHAPTER 5

HINDU SOCIETY

The mores of traditional Hindu society are still upheld in contemporary India. Its embrace is as great now as it ever has been, from the naked wandering ascetic to the sales executive in a Western suit. Worship is performed privately at the home every morning and evening. An abundance of gods and goddesses attract devotion in the temples, with rituals as varied as the bloody sacrifice of a goat and the silent meditation of a yogi.

Despite the great variety of forms of worship and devotion, the underlying bedrock of Hinduism keeps its society in unity. Social responsibilities and a shared religious commitment give Hindus a sense of common purpose and, even for those with little faith, a sense of place within the perceived universe of the Hindu belief system.

THE SYSTEM KNOWN IN THE WEST AS CASTE IS A KEY
PHENOMENON OF TRADITIONAL HINDU SOCIETY. CASTE
AFFECTS WHAT OCCUPATIONS HINDUS FOLLOW, THEIR
CHOICE OF MARRIAGE PARTNERS, WHAT FOOD THEY MUST
EAT, AND MANY OTHER CONSIDERATIONS.

CASTE
THE SYSTEM OF SOCIAL DIVISION

The word *caste* comes from the Portuguese *casta*, "race," but this translation is simplistic and misleading when we look at contemporary Hindu society. In ancient India, society was divided into four categories (varnas, literally "colors"). In descending order of superiority the varnas were Brahmins (priests, teachers), Kshatriyas (rulers, administrators, warriors), Vaishyas (traders, cultivators), and Shudras (servants, laborers). These categories were supposedly based on people's natural qualities. The top three varnas were deemed worthy of learning the Vedas; the Shudras were not. Later, a fifth group was added, originally the pre-Aryan inhabitants of India who were obliged by their masters to carry out "unclean" jobs, such as tanning leather and moving dead

94

LEFT Equality of education in India is one government policy set to undermine the traditional caste system.

OPPOSITE It is still important in most Hindu marriages for the couple, such as this one in Calcutta, to belong to the same caste.

animals. Because their work was dirty and spiritually polluting, this group, termed *outcastes* and formerly known as *untouchables*, had to live in special districts, away from those who did "clean" jobs.

From about 300 B.C.E., the varna framework evolved to contain numerous occupational groups *(jatis)*. In time these jatis became hereditary and exclusive, and can be identified with the "castes" of contemporary India. Distinctive customs developed, and strict rules forbade social interaction with different castes.

Hindus believe they can be polluted by, for example, eating food cooked by a lower caste member, or by drinking water from the same well, whereas low-caste Hindus cannot become more "pure" by associating with the higher castes. In modern India, government attempts to create a fairer society by providing public education and equality of opportunity has undermined the caste system. In the more Westernized cities, eating together and social mixing is normal, but in rural areas caste remains important, especially concerning marriage.

See also "Karma and Rebirth," page 64.

ACCORDING to tradition probably begun in the upanishad period, the life of a Hindu should divide into four stages. An ideal life span of 100 years would break down into four phases (*ashramas*) of about twenty-five years each.

STAGES of LIFE
THE FOUR PHASES TO LIBERATION

The four ashramas are defined as celibate student, married householder, forest recluse, and ascetic wanderer. The ashramas are open only to males belonging to the upper three varnas (see "Caste," page 94) and to women who are qualified in a profession.

Religious tradition dictates that a boy between eight and twelve years old should enter the stage of studentship by attaching himself to a teacher who will instruct him in the Vedas. The boy will live with his teacher

and undergo a ceremony in which he will be invested with the "sacred thread," a symbol of his second, spiritual birth. He will follow religious vows: bathing every morning, offering water to the gods, the sages, and the ancestors, and tending the sacred fire. He also learns to abstain from luxuries, such as meat and honey, as well as from the company of women.

When the "twice-born" young man has completed his studies, he should marry and begin the second ashrama.

He is obliged to have a family, especially sons, and to create wealth by following the vocation of his father's caste. In this second stage the householder is the provider, both for his family and for the other ashramas. Material possessions and also sexual enjoyment are considered honorable goals for the householder.

Having fulfilled his duties as the head of the family, the man may leave his home and retire to the forest in renunciation of the social world, with only the company of his wife if he so chooses. His aim in this is to control his senses and reduce desire, thus paving the way for the fourth stage of complete renunciation in old age. In this final ashrama, living as a homeless ascetic, he will wander from village to village with a begging bowl for food, indifferent to everything around him and concentrating on pursuing oneness with higher Brahman, or God.

In reality, few go beyond the second stage, but leaving home can always be put off until a future life.

See also "Holy Persons," page 98.

LEFT The fourth stage of life, that of the complete ascetic, is the hardest to undergo. While few reach it in a single lifetime, their hope for the salvation of their soul looks to a future incarnation.

ABOVE A wedding marks the beginning of the second ashrama, that of family life.

ALL THOSE WHO WISH TO FIND SALVATION MUST ULTIMATELY
RENOUNCE THE LIFE OF THE WORLD. IN HINDUISM, HOLY
PERSONS (SADHUS) ARE HONORED AS THOSE WHO HAVE
REACHED THIS HIGHEST STAGE OF SPIRITUAL DEVELOPMENT.

HOLY
PERSONS
RENOUNCING THE WORLD

Since all Hindus aspire to reach this ultimate state, the holy hermit is held in high esteem, a sort of spiritual aristocrat, who has risen in status to a position beyond the everyday social order. His or her progress may have taken many ages of fluctuating fortunes through successive incarnations of the soul.

But an individual must feel ready spiritually before he or she can renounce the world. The right time is usually accompanied by a strong feeling about the futility of life. The aspiring holy man or woman leaves home in a solemn ritual, taking to the road as a wandering beggar. With no family obligations, no ritual duties, and no work to do, they rove wherever the spirit takes them—perhaps to temples, religious festivals, and other holy sites.

Because skills developed in the former life do not equip would-be holy persons for their new life, they seek out a guru, a teacher who has

98

already made the mystical journey, from whom they can learn the ways of the inner self. It is believed that destiny will bring about this meeting, at which each will recognize the other.

The guru performs an initiation rite in which the holy disciple formally leaves behind this world and enters the realm of transcendence. His or her queue—the tuft of hair signifying conformity to the Hindu life—is cut off and thereafter the hair grows unkempt. There is no longer any binding to the rules of caste, and even a new personal name is conferred in recognition of their changed existence.

The holy persons will spend their time meditating on the soul within themselves and in all beings, practicing advanced techniques of yoga. They will hope to strip away all sense of their individuality and, while still living, achieve liberation (moksha) in Brahman, the universal consciousness.

ABOVE Sadhus consider nature to be part of God and therefore deem it wrong to cut their hair.

LEFT The only possessions of a wandering holy person may be his clothes, a begging bowl, and a staff.

WOMEN
THEIR ROLE IN HINDUISM

VIEWS ABOUT THE ROLE OF WOMEN IN HINDU INDIA ARE VARIED AND CONTRADICTORY. ALTHOUGH THE TRADITIONAL SUBSERVIENCE OF THE WOMAN TO THE MAN STILL HOLDS IN SOME AREAS, IN HINDU SOCIETY AS A WHOLE THERE IS MUCH THAT POINTS TO THE EQUALITY OF THE SEXES.

ABOVE Hindu women and men participate equally in religious life; both make pilgrimages, visit temples, and offer sacrifices.

Hardly any major areas of Hindu practice remain exclusive to men. A wife is considered the equal of her husband in dharma, and will share his destiny, for which she will fast regularly with her husband. Women conduct the same public offices as men, such as going on pilgrimage, visiting temples, and offering religious sacrifices.

Although the depiction in the *Ramayana* epic of Sita—the devoted and obedient wife of Rama—is the traditional Hindu image of the ideal woman, the reality of everyday relations between husband and wife is usually different. As mistress of the household and mother of its children, she holds considerable authority in the home. She is in charge of ritual purity and leads much of the private worship. The idea that every Hindu woman lives out her life in the shadow of her husband is unrealistic, as this quotation from a Brahmin woman illustrates (from S. Stevenson, *The Rites of the Twice-Born*, 1920):

> In the mornings all I have time to do is to stand at the bottom of his bed and say: "Get up!," and after that I am far too busy cooking for him to have any time to waste in worshipping him!

Traditional laws discriminating against women have been abolished. Girls receive education equal to that of boys. Widows are allowed to remarry. The practice of sati, in which a widow immolates herself on her husband's funeral pyre, was outlawed by Hindu reformers in the nineteenth century, as was child marriage. There are no longer laws to prevent the rise of women to the highest ranks in India, as Indira Gandhi (1917–84) showed by twice becoming prime minister.

BACKGROUND A street scene in a Rajasthani village shows women dressed in traditional fashion.

THE STONE TEMPLES DEDICATED TO HINDU DEITIES ARE
AMONG THE MOST IMPRESSIVE FORMS OF ARCHITECTURE
TO BE FOUND IN THE WORLD. THESE GREAT GRAVITY-
DEFYING STRUCTURES, LIKE SCULPTURED MOUNTAINS, SOAR
INTO THE SKY ALL OVER INDIA.

TEMPLES
ABODES OF THE GODS

At Tanjore, Konarak, Madurai, and Khajuraho—to mention just a few of the great examples—people come to worship because they wish to approach the divine. The temple is the house of a god or goddess. The deity's holy image, in which he or she is believed to reside once various rituals have been performed by priests, is kept in an inner sanctuary at the heart of the temple. But the entire fabric, inside and out, is considered sacred, giving rise to the plethora of sculptured images of deities and mythological figures that adorn the walls in a sometimes bewildering profusion of intricate detail.

BELOW Elaborately sculpted into a wall of the thirteenth-century temple of Konarak is the chariot of Surya, the ancient sun god of the Vedas.

The notion that a deity has a home is not to be taken as a contradiction of the idea that God is everywhere and in all things. The deity may manifest itself in various forms and in various places. For Hindus, worshiping a god means embracing the whole universe in a little object. With emphasis on the personal in Hindu faith, the temple, unlike a church, is not a place for congregational worship. Although rituals are conducted by the temple priests, visitors come at all times of the day to say prayers and to offer gifts of flowers, food, garlands, and ornaments as signs of their devotion to the temple god or goddess.

Throughout the day priests attend to the needs of the deity as though he or she were a living being: the image is regularly bathed, fed, and put to rest, during which time no worshiper may approach.

LEFT The twelfth-century Hoysaleshwara temple at Halebid is renowned for its intricate stone carvings. They depict a vast array of gods and goddesses, as well as hunters, farmers, warriors, musicians, and dancers.

BACKGROUND When Hindus began to travel beyond India, they took their distinctive styles of temple-building with them. The temple of Prambanan was built in the ninth century in Java, Indonesia.

103

FOR HINDUS, WORSHIP (*puja*) takes place as much in the home as in the temple. One room of the house contains images of the gods that the family has chosen to worship. These images may be statues or just pictures, and, in addition, the household may keep images of modern "saints," such as Mahatma Gandhi or even Jesus of Nazareth.

WORSHIP AT HOME

RITES WITHIN THE HOUSEHOLD

ABOVE The puja shrine at home contains various ritual offerings, including turmeric powder, kumkum, rice and other foods, water, incense, and light.

Domestic worship is led by a senior member of the family who must bathe beforehand to be ritually clean. A morning invocation of the sun, repeated several times, is followed by a daily ritual involving the washing and drying of images *(murtis)* of deities, after which they are offered red kumkum and yellow turmeric powders, water, rice grains, flowers, food, incense, and light. A further ritual, known as *arati*, is then performed by passing a ghee lamp (ghee is clarified butter) in front of the images while sacred verses of praise are sung. Food placed before the deities is "received back" as blessed offering *(prasad)*.

Various other rites are performed in the home on a regular basis, including the reverential remembrance of deceased relatives. Important ceremonies marking rites of passage are also conducted in the family home: the birth of a child, initiation as an adult member of the caste and family, marriage, and death all demand the performance of traditional rituals.

See also "Stages of Life," page 96, and "Death and Funerals," page 106.

ABOVE AND LEFT The household will set up icons of deities, such as the elephant god Ganesha, and possibly even images from other religious traditions.

DEATH AND FUNERALS

THE CONTINUANCE OF LIFE

HINDUS BELIEVE THAT AT DEATH ONLY THE BODY
DIES, WHEREAS THE SPIRIT OR SOUL (ATMAN) LIVES MANY
TIMES IN DIFFERENT BODIES UNTIL IT FINDS LIBERATION
(MOKSHA) FROM THE CYCLE OF BIRTH, DEATH, AND REBIRTH.
PROPERLY PERFORMED DEATH RITUALS ARE IMPORTANT IN
RELEASING THE SOUL SO THAT IT MAY CONTINUE ITS
JOURNEY TOWARD LIBERATION.

106

A dying person ideally is given water from the sacred River Ganges and encouraged to utter God's name, usually "Ram Ram," so that the soul can attain peace. When he or she dies, the corpse is bathed and dressed in new clothes. All adult relations then enter a state of ritual impurity for ten days. The men in the family prepare a stretcher made of bamboo staves. After placing the corpse on it, they cover the body with a new white cloth and red flowers, and tie it securely. By tradition, the eldest or the youngest son, who carries live coals in an earthen pot, walks in front of the corpse as it is carried to the funeral ground near a local river.

Hindus cremate their dead, but very young babies and wandering holy men *(sannyasins)* are buried. When the pyre has been constructed and the corpse placed on it, the son performs his religious duty of lighting it while the priest chants mantras (sacred verses) to sanctify the fire. Then the son walks around it three or five or seven times, holding a burning torch.

Sometimes a small hole is drilled in the earthen pot, which is then filled with water. As the son walks around the pyre, dripping water forms a limiting line to prevent the soul from returning as a ghost. When the heat cracks the skull of the corpse, the mourners bathe in the river and return home, leaving the cremation-ground staff to tend the pyre. On the third day after the cremation, the ashes are collected, and after the tenth day, they are cast into a holy river.

LEFT Hindu funeral rituals, such as this cremation beside the River Ganges in the holy city of Varanasi, are important. Their proper conduct will help release the soul from its confinement within the body.

The cow holds a special place in Hinduism. Ancient scriptures associate it with various deities, including Devi, the Mother Goddess. The venerable creature is seen as a symbol of life itself, of all creation, and of the earth in its capacity to produce food and nourishment.

THE
SACRED COW
REVERENCE FOR LIFE

In ancient India the *Bhagavata Purana* narrates the adventures of the youthful god Krishna, who leads an idyllic pastoral existence as a cowherd. To worship the cow is to follow Krishna's example.

It comes as no surprise, then, that to kill or harm these sacred animals is prohibited. The sin of killing a cow is equal to murdering a Brahmin, a member of the highest priestly caste. Indeed, cows are so revered that they are allowed to wander as they wish, even in the most densely populated of Indian cities.

The logical extension to this respect for the cow is that all life is sacred, and that no animal should be killed unnecessarily, certainly not violently. Although in ancient India oxen and bulls were sacrificed and eaten, today almost all Hindus are vegetarian. Orthodox Hindus make sure that their food is prepared in accordance with strict dietary laws in order to maintain ritual purity. Cows are also valued for their nutritious milk and for their dung, which can be used as a fuel and which becomes a purifying agent when mixed with water.

ABOVE Revered as sacred among animals, the cow is free to roam wherever it pleases. Mahatma Gandhi said it represents all India.

LEFT Cows were at the heart of Hindu stories about Krishna, a cowherd, disporting with the local dairymaids.

GURUS
THE SPIRITUAL TEACHERS

IN ANCIENT TIMES SAGES WERE BELIEVED TO HAVE HEARD
GOD'S REVEALED WORD (THE VEDIC SCRIPTURES ARE CALLED
SHRUTI, MEANING "THAT WHICH IS HEARD"). THEY PASSED ON
THE VEDAS AND OTHER LORE TO GURUS, WISE TEACHERS
ENTRUSTED WITH THE TASK OF MEMORIZING AND
INTERPRETING THE SACRED HYMNS.

ABOVE Mohandas Gandhi was called Mahatma, meaning "Great Soul." He was a charismatic spiritual leader
described as "a saint of action rather than contemplation."

RIGHT One influential teacher who today has centers all over the world was Shri Baba of Haidakhan. A hermit
who lived in a cave in the Himalayas in the 1970s and 1980s, he taught that the essence of all things is love.

For centuries the Hindu scriptures were transmitted orally from one generation to the next without ever a word being written down. Itinerant gurus brought the great epics of Hindu literature, the *Mahabharata* and the *Ramayana*, to village folk who could not read Sanskrit.

How crucial, therefore, the role of the guru was, and how awesome his figure! He is still held in exalted status. A Hindu student is expected to show great respect to the guru, who confers immortality through his wisdom.

Traditionally, at the age of twelve, a male is initiated into the religion and mentored by a guru to learn the Vedas and other scriptures. In some sects the guru instructs the initiate in a secret mantra, as well as in rituals and meditations.

The yoga systems were handed down and taught by gurus. Modern gurus, such as the Maharishi Mahesh Yogi, who founded the Transcendental Meditation movement (see "Modern Hindu Cults," page 124), continue to use the oral method in teaching their followers. Since the 1980s, gurus have become "electronic," using modern technology to transmit their message.

FOR HINDUS, PILGRIMAGE IS SUCH AN IMPORTANT FEATURE
OF THEIR RELIGION THAT ALMOST ANYWHERE IN INDIA CAN
BE CONSIDERED HOLY ENOUGH TO BE A FOCUS FOR
PILGRIMS. THE NUMBER OF PILGRIMAGE SITES MAY
VARIOUSLY BE COUNTED BETWEEN 58 AND 64,000, DEPENDING
ON THE CRITERION USED.

PILGRIMAGE
SACRED JOURNEYS

Holy places, for Hindus, are usually by a river or coast, or on a mountain. A place might assume a special significance if there is a historical or legendary association. Thus Varanasi (Benares) is where the god Shiva manifested himself, and it is also associated with Rama, an incarnation of Vishnu.

Special times attract pilgrims. Every year during the Dusserah farming festival in October, the story of the *Ramayana* is enacted in a cycle lasting thirty days. At Vrindaban, pilgrims gather at the time of the spring equinox in the hope of seeing a vision of Krishna disporting with his friends, the cow maidens. Modern places of pilgrimage include the cremation site of Mahatma Gandhi near the bank of the Jumna (or Yamuna) river in Delhi.

Pilgrimage can be a great equalizer. In the Ganges, the holiest river in India, the pure are made even more pure, and the impure have their pollution removed, if only temporarily. Immersed in the sacred water, and perhaps anywhere in the holy cities

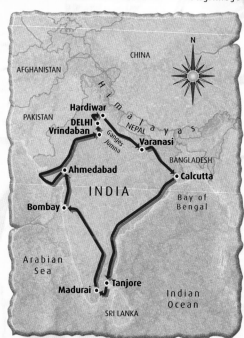

Many Hindus undertake an all-India pilgrimage by train (route indicated on the map), which takes about ten weeks.

of Varanasi or Hardiwar, distinctions of caste are supposed to count for nothing. Although caste is thought to be divinely ordained, it has no eternal significance, and the sincere pilgrim, regardless of caste, is held to enter eternity at least for the time of the pilgrimage.

The value of a pilgrimage in terms of merit depends on the way it is regarded by the devotee. Some Hindus consider merit to be reckoned by the distance that has been traveled, the means of transport (walking is best), the auspiciousness of the timing, and the holiness of the place. Most hold pilgrimage in great honor, endeavoring to mirror the geographical journey with an inner spiritual one.

BACKGROUND At dawn, pilgrims perform *sandyhas* (personal meditations) on the banks of the Ganges to mark an important stage in the sun's daily passage.

KUMBHA MELA

THE GREATEST FESTIVAL

IN JANUARY 2001, SOME TWENTY-FIVE MILLION PEOPLE ASSEMBLED AT PRAYAG NEAR ALLAHABAD IN NORTHERN INDIA TO CELEBRATE THE MAHA ("GREAT") KUMBHA MELA FESTIVAL. OCCURING JUST ONCE EVERY TWELVE YEARS, IT IS THE MOST SACRED OF ALL THE HINDU PILGRIMAGES. TENS OF THOUSANDS OF SAINTS, MONKS, AND HOLY MEN JOINED OTHER PILGRIMS IN A VAST SPECTACLE OF RITUAL BATHING, MASS FEEDING, SINGING, PRAYER, AND RELIGIOUS DEBATE.

ABOVE Pilgrimage can be a great equalizer. While bathing in the sacred River Ganges, distinctions of caste count for nothing and the impure lose their pollution, if only temporarily.

It is thought that people have been communing here since as long ago as the fourth millennium B.C.E. A confluence of three sacred rivers—the Ganges, Jumna, and the invisible Saraswati—form the focus for devotees of many faiths who believe that during the Kumbha Mela the waters contain divine properties capable of banishing evil. By bathing in them, pilgrims believe, they may attain salvation. During the two months of the festival there are certain auspicious dates when, according to astrologers, these waters are charged with positive energy and pilgrims descend to the rivers to bathe. The dating of the festival is determined by the arrival of the planet Jupiter in Aquarius and the sun in Aries.

The name Kumbha Mela means "festival of the pot," and derives from Hindu mythology. The story tells of gods churning the sea into a milky froth to produce an elixir *(amrit)* to bring eternal life. A demon snatched the precious drink and in the ensuing chase, which lasted twelve days (the equivalent of twelve human years), four drops of the nectar spilled to earth. The places where the holy ambrosia landed are now the four sites—Prayag near Allahabad (for the "Maha" festival), Hardiwar, Ujjain, and Nasik—where the festival is celebrated in a cycle lasting twelve years.

BACKGROUND The Kumbha Mela festival at Allahabad is a joyous occasion when millions of sadhus (holy men) and ordinary people from all walks of life make their way to the banks of the River Ganges.

115

HINDUISM

IN the WORLD

From as early as the second century of the common era Hinduism was known in Southeast Asia. Hindu priests traveling with Indian traders to Indonesia established their religion in many of the islands, especially Java and Bali.

During the past hundred years, many Hindus, most of them economic migrants, have moved westward. Today, these migrants are to be found especially in Britain and countries of the British Commonwealth, such as the Caribbean, Canada, and eastern Africa, as well as in the United States and Europe. In recent times, one of the most visible groups with its roots in Hinduism has been the Hare Krishna movement.

SWAMI VIVEKANANDA

HINDUISM COMES TO THE WEST

At the WORLD PARLIAMENT OF RELIGIONS HELD IN 1893 IN CHICAGO, ONE MAN CREATED SUCH A STIR THAT THE WORLD'S APPRECIATION OF HINDUISM WAS FOREVER CHANGED. AN INDIAN HOLY PERSON, SWAMI VIVEKANANDA, PRESENTED HIS FAITH TO THE ASSEMBLY IN A WAY THAT NO HINDU HAD DONE BEFORE. THE APPEAL AND GOOD SENSE OF THE FAITH HE ESPOUSED IMPRESSED NOT ONLY FELLOW BELIEVERS BUT INTERESTED AGNOSTICS, TOO.

ABOVE The liberal-minded missionary Vivekananda was the first person to establish a genuine cross-cultural interaction between Hinduism and twentieth-century America.

As the first great Hindu missionary to the West, Vivekananda founded an order of monks, the Ramakrishna Mission, named after Ramakrishna Paramahansa, whose deep spirituality had a powerful effect on all he met. This man's claim to be able to see God in every person and in every religion laid the basis of Vivekananda's mission. Vivekananda followed his master's belief in the Vedantic teaching of pure monism (see "Vedanta Philosophy," page 68), the idea that all reality is of God and consists of the same one substance. He regarded Hinduism as the mother of all religions, all of which were true, and said that we should all follow our own in search of God. He also emphasized that we had a duty to look after our fellow human beings, and to reduce their suffering wherever possible.

Vivekananda's form of Hinduism, which demanded no belief in a personal creator god, found wide appeal among the educated and liberal sectors of society, including the writer Aldous Huxley. Through Vivekananda's interpretation, Hinduism was perceived to be rational and morally respectable. After 1897 his Vedanta societies grew rapidly in both India and America, and set the pattern for the existence of Hinduism in America. Many other charismatic Hindus followed in his footsteps, and centers of Hinduism became permanently established in the West.

Vivekananda's views were developed by his disciple Sarvepalli Radhakrishnan, a professor of religion, who believed that Hinduism had a mission to bring together the peoples of the world into a healing unity. He prophesied that the world's religions would dissolve into a new monistic faith. Some Hindus today take Radhakrishnan's neo-Vedantic vision to be the ground of modern Hindu orthodoxy.

BACKGROUND The handprint of Swami Vivekananda.

THE
HARE KRISHNA
MOVEMENT

KNOWN FORMALLY AS THE INTERNATIONAL SOCIETY
FOR KRISHNA CONSCIOUSNESS (ISKCON), HARE KRISHNA
WAS FOUNDED IN THE UNITED STATES IN 1966 BY
A.C. BHAKTIVEDANTA SWAMI (1896–1977). ONCE A SUCCESSFUL
BUSINESSMAN IN BENGAL, HE BECAME A MISSIONARY
AND SETTLED IN LOS ANGELES TO PREACH A SIDE OF
HINDUISM PREVIOUSLY UNFAMILIAR TO AMERICANS.

HARE KRISHNA HARE KRISHNA, KRISHNA KRISHNA, HA

KRISH

The teachings of Bhaktivedanta were based on those of a Bengali guru, Caitanya (1486–1533), who in turn drew his inspiration from the beliefs of the *Bhagavad Gita*, which dates back to before the common era. ISKCON followers practice a form of Bhakti yoga, devotion to a personal god through love, in which the emphasis of worship is on Krishna rather than on Vishnu, from whom he emanated. Followers believe that through this worship Krishna incarnates himself in individuals.

The principal form of devotion is the group chanting of the names of God. The main mantra, or sacred verse, is the maha mantra:

The chanting of this mantra by followers gave the movement its popular name Hare Krishna. There is also devotional service, which involves collective worship and activities such as teaching, cooking, and distributing literature in return for donations.

Followers are initiated at a Hare Krishna temple in a ceremony that binds the disciple to a guru for life. The novice vows to observe the principles of Krishna consciousness: abstinence from meat, fish, eggs, and intoxicants; avoidance of sexual relations, except within marriage, and then only for procreation; no gambling; and daily sessions of chanting and reading from the works of the founder.

See also "Bhakti Yoga," page 88.

HARE KRISHNA HARE KRISHNA,
KRISHNA KRISHNA,
HARE HARE;
HARE RAMA HARE RAMA,
RAMA RAMA,
HARE HARE.

OPPOSITE The Hare Krishna movement provides popular day centers for poor children in India.

e HaRe HaRe Rama HaRe Rama, Rama, HaRe HaRe

FAITHS RELATED TO HINDUISM
JAINISM, BUDDHISM, SIKHISM

IN INDIA, CERTAIN GROUPS EMERGED BY WAY OF REACTION
TO MAINSTREAM HINDUISM, AND DEVELOPED INTO MAJOR
RELIGIONS IN THEIR OWN RIGHT. SOME HINDUS, HOWEVER,
STILL REGARD THEM AS BELONGING TO THE HINDU FOLD.

J ainism and Buddhism appeared in the sixth century B.C.E. in protest against the sacrificial system and the authority of the Brahmin priests. Both sects contended that rituals and icons were of no use in overcoming the basic problem of samsara, the cycle of birth, death, and rebirth.

A non-Brahmin prince, Vardhamana, later known as Mahavira ("Great Hero"), founded Jainism, which takes its name from *Jinas,* or Conquerors—those who have won the victory of enlightenment. Mahavira lived a life of extreme austerity, eating little, keeping silent, and meditating intensely. Through such practice, he was deemed to have halted the accumulation of karma, good or bad, and to have achieved enlightenment. His followers hope that, by removing the acts that create karma, they too may be liberated from bondage to the material world.

Like Mahavira, Siddharta Gautama (later called "the Buddha," or "Enlightened One") rejected the Vedas and left home to seek enlightenment. After six years, he found *Nirvana,* the ultimate state of pure being. For Buddhists, Nirvana is found not by worshiping a personal creator god, but by developing morality, meditation, and wisdom. Driven from India by reactionary Brahmanical Hinduism, Buddhism spread southward to Southeast Asia and northward through the Himalayas to Nepal and Tibet, and thence to China.

The founder of Sikhism, Guru Nanak, was born into a Hindu family in 1469. He taught about the importance to all Hindus and Muslims of three things: meditation, honest toil, and almsgiving. More this-worldly than Hindus, Sikhs believe the everyday world is real, not an illusion. Like Hindus, Sikhs maintain that the soul is reborn after death, and that, by living a God-centered life, people can attain liberation from rebirth in their current existence through God's grace.

LEFT The nature of Hinduism is so embracing that even followers of radical new movements, such as the ten gurus of Sikhism, still regarded themselves as Hindus.

THE RESPECT FOR THEIR FAITH AND OUTLOOK THAT
CHARISMATIC HINDU FIGURES SUCH AS MAHATMA GANDHI
HAVE CREATED IN MODERN TIMES HAS MAINTAINED THE
WEST'S INTEREST IN THIS OLDEST OF LIVING RELIGIONS. IN
TURN, THIS INTEREST HAS ENCOURAGED THE GROWTH OF
NEW EXPRESSIONS OF HINDUISM.

MODERN HINDU CULTS
TM AND SAI BABA

One of the first and best-known of the new Hindu cults, although it regards itself as more of a technique than a religion, transcendental meditation (known colloquially as TM) was started in India in 1958 by a monk, Maharishi Mahesh Yogi (c. 1911–). Trained as a physicist, the Maharishi began teaching his philosophy in the West, his aim being to improve through meditation both the individual and society in general. The movement grew slowly in the West until it was popularized by the pop group The Beatles in the late 1960s. Since then, it has developed its meditation-based program known as the Science of Creative Intelligence.

TM has a simple initiation rite, during which members are given a secret Sanskrit mantra upon which they meditate daily, to induce deep relaxation, leading to greater vitality and creativity. TM also runs

courses in which various techniques and powers, including levitation, are said to be acquired. The movement maintains that the effectiveness of its techniques can be proved scientifically. (See also "Mantra Yoga," page 80.)

Another successful new Indian cult, which also spread in the late 1960s, was the Sai Baba Movement. The cult is named after its founder, Sathya Sai Baba (1926–), who acquired a reputation as a miracle worker and claims to be the reincarnation of the holy man Sai Baba of Shirdi (c. 1856–1918). The movement's teachings differ little from those of mainstream Hinduism, but in particular they stress adherence to the Vedic scriptures and the avoidance of materialistic thinking. Most devotees will also try to attend an audience with Sai Baba, held at the movement's headquarters in Prasanthi Nilayam in India.

LEFT Sai Baba, who lives at the movement's headquarters in India, commands great devotion from followers.

ABOVE Maharishi Mahesh Yogi brought Hindu meditation into the limelight with his conversion of The Beatles.

GLOSSARY

arati ritual waving of ghee lamps

ashram spiritual retreat

ashrama one of the four stages in life—student, householder, recluse, or wanderer

atman the eternal self, or soul, of an individual

avatara descent or incarnation of God (notably of Vishnu)

bhakti loving devotion to God

Brahman sacred Power in the cosmos; the Divine Being

chakra one of seven spiritual centers of the body

deva a god or divine power

dharma pattern that underlies the cosmos, seen in social and ethical laws

dukkha suffering or grief

guru teacher of spiritual matters

jati caste; occupational social group, hereditary and exclusive

jnana path of knowledge

karma law governing the effects of deeds in this life and the next

mandala geometric design used in meditation

mantra sacred name or syllable, used in spiritual practice

maya Brahman's power of illusion

moksha liberation of the soul

murti image of a deity

prasad blessed offering at worship

puja worship

rita Vedic principle giving order and rhythm to the universe

sadhu holy person or saint

samsara cycle of birth, death, and rebirth of the soul

sannyasin person who has renounced the world, usually wandering

sati widow's self-immolation on her husband's funeral pyre

siddhi psychic power

varna one of four social categories in ancient India

INDEX

FURTHER READING

Chatterjii, J., *Wisdom of the Vedas*,
Wheaton: Quest Books, 1992

Cotterell, A., *A Dictionary of World
Mythology*, New York: Oxford
University Press, 1986

Crim, K. (ed.), *Abingdon Dictionary
of Living Religions*, Nashville:
Abingdon, 1981

Fenton, J.Y., Hein, N., Reynolds
F.E., Miller, A.L., Nielsen, C.,

Religions of Asia, New York: St
Martin's Press, 1983

Gandhi, M., *An Autobiography: The
Story of My Experiments with Truth*,
Washington DC: Public Affairs
Press, 1948

Hinnells, J. (ed.), *A Handbook of
Living Religions*, New York: Viking
Penguin, 1984

Knapp, S., *Secret Teachings of the
Vedas*, Detroit: The World Relief
Network, 1990

Mascaro, J., *The Upanishads*, New
York: Penguin Books, 1965

Sharma, I., *Dharma Deck: Wisdom
from the Vedas*, San Rafael (CA):
Mandala Publishing Group, 2002

Sidharth, B. *Celestial Key to the
Vedas: Discovering the Origins of the
World's Oldest Civilization*, Rochester
(Vermont): Inner Traditions, 1999

Sivaraman, K., (ed.) *Hindu
Spirituality I: Vedas Through
Vedanta* (World Spirituality series),
New York: The Crossroad
Publishing Co., 1986

CREDITS

Key: t = top, b = bottom, l = left,
r = right, b/g = background

Quarto would like to thank and
acknowledge the following for images
reproduced in this book:

2: Patrick O'Sullivan; 3: Heritage
Images/The British Library; 4–5b: Patrick
O'Sullivan; 7b: Patrick O'Sullivan; 10:
Ann Ronan Picture Library; 10–11b/g:
Art Directors and TRIP; 12: Art
Directors and TRIP/H Rogers; 12–13b/g:
Art Directors and TRIP/Dinodia; 15t:
Heritage Images/The British Library;
15b: Art Directors and TRIP/Resource
Foto; 16: Ann Ronan Picture Library;
16–17: Ann Ronan Picture Library; 19:
Art Directors and TRIP/Dinodia; 20:
Heritage Images/The British Museum;
21: Fiona Robertson; 22–23b/g: Art
Directors and TRIP/Dinodia; 23: Fiona
Robertson; 27: Art Directors and
TRIP/Ask Images; 28: Heritage
Images/The British Library; 29: Heritage
Images/The British Library; 30: Art
Directors and TRIP/H Rogers; 31: Art
Directors and TRIP/H Rogers; 32: Art
Directors and TRIP/Dinodia; 33: Art
Directors and TRIP/Dinodia; 35: Ann
Ronan Picture Library; 35b/g: Ann
Ronan Picture Library; 36: Art Directors
and TRIP/C Wormald; 37: Corbis; 42t:
Ann Ronan Picture Library; 43t:
Heritage Images/The British Library;
43b/g: Heritage Images/The British
Museum; 45: Ann Ronan Picture
Library; 47: Art Directors and TRIP/H
Rogers; 48: Art Directors and TRIP/H
Rogers; 50: Art Directors and TRIP/H
Rogers; 51: Ann Ronan Picture Library;
54: Art Directors and TRIP/H Rogers;
55: Art Directors and TRIP; 57: Ann
Ronan Picture Library; 58: Corbis; 59:
Heritage Images/The British Museum;
63: Ann Ronan Picture Library; 64: Art
Directors and TRIP/H Rogers; 67l: Fiona
Robertson; 67r: Fiona Robertson; 68:
Art Directors and TRIP/H Rogers; 72:
Corbis; 74: Heritage Images/The British
Library; 77: Heritage Images/The British
Library; 78: Art Directors and TRIP/
Resource Foto; 83: Corbis; 84: Heritage
Images/The British Library; 85: Corbis;
87: Fiona Robertson; 89: Art Directors
and TRIP/C Wormald; 93: Art Directors
and TRIP/H Rogers; 94: Art Directors
and TRIP/H Rogers; 95: Art Directors
and TRIP/H Rogers; 96: Corbis; 97:
Heritage Images/The British Library; 98:
Fiona Robertson; 99: Art Directors and
TRIP/H Rogers; 100: Art Directors and
TRIP/B Turner; 100–101b/g Ingeborg
Shea; 102: Fiona Robertson; 103: Ann
Ronan Picture Library; 104: Art
Directors and TRIP/F Good; 106: Art
Directors and TRIP/H Rogers; 108: Art
Directors and TRIP/C Wormald; 109:
Fiona Robertson; 110: Ann Ronan
Picture Library; 111: Art Directors and
TRIP/H Rogers; 112–113b/g: Art
Directors and TRIP/H Rogers; 114:
Art Directors and TRIP /Dinodia; 114–
115b/g: Art Directors and TRIP/Dinodia;
117: Topham Picturepoint; 118: Topham
Picturepoint; 119: Topham Picturepoint;
120: Art Directors and TRIP/C Wormald;
122: Art Directors and TRIP/H Rogers;
124: Topham Picturepoint; 125: Topham
Picturepoint

All other illustrations are the copyright of
Quarto. While every effort has been made
to credit contributors, we apologize should
there have been any omissions or errors.

051952586